Artist, writer, adventurer, ~~~~~~~ ~~~
Desmond Doig was a Renaissance Man, who spent his life creating.

As a roving reporter at *The Statesman,* he created investigative journalism in India. As special correspondent, he travelled through India to the Himalayan kingdoms and into the Himalayas themselves. He wrote about Bhutan for *National Geographic* before anyone else did and took photographs for *Life* about Nepal. He adventured into the Nepal Himalayas as scribe for The Edmund Hillary Expedition and searched for the Yeti and climbed Mount Makalu.

He authored *High in the Thin Cold Air* with Sir Edmund Hillary; a book on Sikkim, *Calcutta: An Artist's Impression; Mother Teresa: Her work and Her People,* which have been translated into thirty-two languages. Desmond Doig designed gardens, hotels, interiors, clothes and campaigns for films.

When he died in 1983, Desmond was working on *An Artist's Impression of Delhi,* and *An Artist's Impression of Goa.* He was also planning an autobiography of sixty-three years of a rich, varied and vibrant life.

Dubby Bhagat has been a salesman, a journalist, and advertising copywriter, a guide and a hotelier in The Everest Hotel, Nepal's premier five-star property.

With his mentor Desmond Doig, he helped to design The Malla Hotel and The Shangri-la. And he helped Desmond to write *Mother Teresa: Her Work and Her People* and *My Kind of Kathmandu.*

He has written *Peak Hour* with his adopted son A.D. Sherpa and is working on a book about walks in Kathmandu with journalist John Child.

He lives in Kathmandu with his son, his daughter-in-law Lhamu Sherpa and grandchildren Duksangh and Heyshe.

In the Kingdom of the Gods

An artist's impression of the emerald valley

Desmond Doig
Based on research by
Dubby Bhagat

HarperCollins *Publishers* India

HarperCollins *Publishers* India Pvt Ltd
7/16 Ansari Road, Daryaganj, New Delhi 110 002

Published 1999 by
HarperCollins *Publishers* India

ISBN 81-7223-371-X

Typeset in Calisto MT by
Nikita Overseas Pvt. Ltd.
19-A, Ansari Road, Daryaganj
New Delhi 110 002

Printed in India by
Gopsons Papers Ltd
A-14, Sector 60
Noida 201 301

Were Desmond with us he would have dedicated this book to Kathmandu saying it was, "always changing, ever the same, inevitably fascinating".

...and he would have approved of my dedicating it at the close of the millennium to the people who took over the difficult task of looking after me, Utpal and Caroline Sengupta and the two who bore the brunt of my troublesome ways, the always understanding industrialist M.A. Lari and his wondrous wife Najma.

To Kalyani, Shanti, Yasmin and Arniko who have kept faith and whose expanding empire of shops all bear Desmond's name.

And as usual to my mother Mohini Bhagat who sent cucumber sandwiches and love to Kathmandu while this book was being written.

Also to A.D. Sherpa, John Child, Ram Thapa, Pasang Temba and other Friends In High Places. Desmond's pictures adorn their websites.

To Mikki McRee, who in her Reach For The Sky, brings comfort and company to Nepal, and who in selling The Himalayas, borrows extensively from Desmond.

Contents

Foreword

It was the writer Sunanda Dutta Ray who said that Desmond found his soul while he did *An Artist's Impression of Calcutta*. What Desmond Doig found as he sketched Kathmandu, was happiness.

I'm not sure which is more important.

M.J. Akbar commissioned the *Kingdom of The Gods* column in a paper he edited at the time. This was many years after Desmond commissioned M.J. to do pieces for the *JS*. What goes around, comes around.

The sketches are in fact the history; the culture and the essence of Nepal all captured in deft lines and words that have a ring of immortality about them.

Desmond did a sketch a week, then down to the post office to send them off. In time the people at the post office became friends who often dropped into the house for tea asking to see the printed article. And we'd tell them the stories we had uncovered that accompanied the drawing.

... and what stories they were.

The god of wood who secured release from tantric spells by promising building material for a temple from a single celestial tree. The king who was doomed to dance till he died. The queen who commanded the death of virtually all of Nepal's nobility. The prince who was ordered to kill his father by the father himself. The princess who took Buddhism to Tibet. The ogre who ate children...

Desmond was delighted by the stories and came to believe it was these legends that kept the fabric of Nepali culture together, religion having become much too complex for the ordinary folk.

It was our publisher who took the sketches away to be published.

And it was Sanjana Malhotra who put it all together.

I wish they'd been with us, all of them, when we went into a Durbar Square or a narrow street or a Rana palace armed with pens that smudged, a drawing book, chocolates and questions, questions, questions.

Because we drew our stories as much from local folklore as we did from the few books on Nepal available at the time.

The stories and much else about the valley were interpreted and garnered by Shanti Singh, the Nepali wife of Desmond's protégé, Kalyan. Shanti, heavy with child, would talk to Desmond about the Kathmandu she knew. Desmond lapped it all up and transformed it into the magic that is about to envelop you. He decided that Shanti's first baby would be called Yasmin after a favoured poem and the second, Arniko, after the creator of the pagoda roof who took his secret to China and beyond.

Yasmin was born just days after Desmond died and Arniko came to be several years later. With these sketches, and the incredible knowledge that goes with them, one hopes they will realise what a wonderful heritage they come from, and what a gem their mother Shanti will forever be and how invaluable she was to this work.

Desmond Doig died in 1983.
Kathmandu changed.

Of an evening, leave well-trodden paths and seek out the winding alley or follow the tap-tap of artisans' hammers and come across an unchanged Desmond sketch come to life. It's all there still waiting to be rediscovered and despite time, the old Kathmandu still has the same fascination to the beholder that it did for the people who first envisioned and then created it.

The Light of Many Suns

 In the beginning, when gods walked the valley of Kathmandu, there was a mound where the temple now stands, and to it daily came a cow to offer her milk. A bewildered cowherd who watched this incredible happening in great awe and fear, at last found the courage to dig at the spot. He had hardly begun when he was consumed by a light like that of many suns emanating from a *linga* with faces of Shiva carved on all four sides. So terrifying was one of the faces that an early invader of the valley looked upon it and died.

There ends the myth and history tentatively begins. Pashupatinath, however small the original shrine, was there when the first settlers raised a perishable town of wood and mud about it on the banks of the sacred Baghmati. The earliest remains are Licchavi, from AD 300 to 800. Licchavi rulers were in close relationship with Gupta India, so Sanskrit was the court language with a growing interest in Hinduism.

Chinese representatives of the time, visiting the Kathmandu valley, described the fabulous court, carved and ornamented with pearls and gems, as being near the holy temple of Pashupatinath, where the king daily worshipped the deity that protected him.

Long before, when the Mauryan king Ashoka visited the valley, he married his daughter Charumati to a local prince and they founded the city of Dev Patan, close to the most sacred shrine. In the fourteenth century the temple was shattered by the invading army of Ghiyas-ud-din Tughlak: three hundred years later it was eaten through by termites.

King Pratap Malla, in atonement for having seduced a minor girl, added a courtyard filled with Shiva lingas. The last Malla king of Kathmandu stripped the temple of all its gold and had it melted down to finance his war against the invading Gurkhas. Such is the power of Pashupatinath, believe the devout, that he lost the battle.

Pashupatinath, as Shiva in one of his many incarnations, is a protector of animals, so there are no sacrifices at this great shrine. Appropriately, throngs of gossiping monkeys swarm through the temples, feasting off votive offerings and sometimes exploding into violent battles that zoom to and fro across the river, up and down stairs scattering pilgrims, along the ghats, and through rows of temples. They live on the wooded hill which is part of the temple complex which reaches the airport, until recently called Gaucher, the meadow of cows.

When I first came to Kathmandu, a famed mystic, the Shivpuri Baba, lived on Pashupati hill in a small hut that seemed part of the forest. I went to meet him and was enchanted by a jovial old man with a flowing beard who claimed to be 150 years old. Lest I doubted him he said he remembered Queen Victoria being crowned empress of India, and had seen the first train in India.

Today, Pashupatinath is a two-tiered pagoda temple with heavily gilded roofs, heavy silver doors that are closed to non-Hindus, and is the centre of a vast conglomeration of temples, shrines, *dharamshalas,* bathing and burning ghats held together by an aura of religious fervour and the smoke from funeral pyres. Here is beauty commissioned by art's greatest patron, religion, so that hardly a stone is unchiselled or wood

uncarved. The windows of even the humblest *dharamshalas* are ornamented with wasp-waist deities and intricate floral designs. Temple spires writhe with golden serpents, and on two of the platforms on which the dead are cremated are sixth century stone carvings of rare beauty.

Two festivals blaze in Pashupatinath more brightly than the others; Shivaratri, when thousands converge on the temple from all over Nepal and India, thronging the area, day and night, and raising shelters and shops wherever space permits. Devotional music is everywhere. At Tij, women from all over the valley walk to the great shrine, married women in their vivid marriage saris and unmarried girls in their brightest best, singing and dancing as they go to bathe in the sacred river and pray at the great temple: the married women for their husbands, the girls for a good and kindly match.

They pour from the temple down the stairway to the river like a burst of scarlet sequins overflowing the ghats and spilling into the water. In their midst, on a stark stone slab, her feet in the water, an old woman in white lies dying. No one apparently bothers but that is what Pashupatinath is all about, destroyer and protector, both. The eternal riddle of life and death.

Every morning Radio Nepal opens its programme with a prayer to Pashupatinath and when the king, himself a reincarnation of Vishnu, addresses his people, he calls upon Pashupatinath to bless and protect them all.

Of Divine Street Walkers

Gods no longer walk the streets of Kathmandu, or if they do, there is an insufficiency of powerful tantrics to recognize them, or perhaps the cosmopolitan crowds make recognition impossible.

Indra, the Lord of Heaven, himself visited Kathmandu to steal flowers from a garden for his mother's devotions, but was discovered and taken captive. While his elephant searched the city for him, his mother descended from heaven to find her son, and when she disclosed to the people who their prisoner was there was much apology, much rejoicing and the inevitable asking for a boon.

Probably the last occasion of deities mingling with humans in Kathmandu was in the early seventeenth century when the celestial tree Kalpavriksha, came in human form to witness a festival. A wily tantric saw through his disguise and bound him with a spell which he was prepared to break if Kalpavriksha promised wood from the celestial tree from which to build a large building. The promise was made and kept. A huge three-floor pagoda building of unusual design was constructed, perhaps as a monastery or *dharamshala* or a temple, no one is quite sure. Certainly it was never consecrated, though today there is an image of Gorakhnath at the centre of the ground floor.

Gorakhnath was a great Shivaite sage who is connected with many wondrous legends. By meditating at the entrance to the hole of the Serpent King, who brought rain to the valley, he caused great drought and pestilence. Centuries later, he was meditating in a cave below the palace of the Gurkha, when the child Prithvi Narayan Shah, who was to become the first king of undivided Nepal, interrupted him. The sage rose to meet the boy and regurgitated in his hands, commanding the boy to eat. The young prince refused and dropped the mess to the ground where it splashed his feet.

If he had eaten as commanded, the saint said, there would have been nothing the prince couldn't have achieved. However, since the sacred vomit had touched his feet, they would lead him to success wherever they went, a prophecy that came true. Gorakhnath today is patron saint of the king and Gurkhas.

Not only was the wood from the celestial tree sufficient to build a large house at the very centre of Kathmandu but there was enough left over with which to construct several other houses in the area. They all stand to this day, at their centre the Kashta Mandap, the house of wood, from which the city of Kathmandu is supposed to have taken its name.

All three stories are open sided with railed balconies on which wandering ascetics or pilgrims could rest. On the first floor are two panels that illustrate the life of the Buddha, which could suggest a Buddhist beginning. However, in the valley of Kathmandu, Buddhism and Hinduism coexist so closely that from the time it was built, between 1620 and 1639, the house cf wood was probably intended for people of all beliefs.

There are, in close proximity to the Kashta Mandap, a dwelling for Buddhist priests with a stunning painted door at its entrance, several votive Buddhist *chaityas,* great stone Garuda and Hindu temples, the most famous of which is the Ashok Binayak, worshipped by both Hindus and Buddhists.

Strangely, this entirely gilded temple has no finial: it is open to the skies in commemoration of two beliefs. One is that the shrine was originally under an Ashoka tree which grew out of its roof. The other is that Ganesh was seen levitating under the tree and so the temple made provision for him to come and go through the roof.

Whatever the real reason, there it stands today, within a few feet of the Kashta Mandap and considered so sacred that the king comes in procession to pray there immediately after his coronation at the old palace, a short distance away. The present king walked to the shrine while thousands watched from the high plinths of temples near the Kashta Mandap.

Indians know the Kashta Mandap well. It was where, in the film *Hare Rama, Hare Krishna,* Zeenat Aman danced while assorted hippies pulled on *chillums* and the famous *Dum Maro Dum* was born.

The Stupa of a Million Dewdrops

 One of the most fabulous places in the fabled valley, is the great Buddhist stupa of Boudhanath. Its huge white dome, surmounted on three enormous tiers, shaped like *mandalas* and supporting a gilded tower and golden finial, create an image as restful as it is vast. It can be seen from all over the valley, a shimmering beacon of faith.

The all-seeing eyes of the compassionate Buddha gaze cobalt, white and scarlet from the gilded sides of the tower, above them a *tikka* and between them, where the nose should be, a question mark that, no matter what it means, for me enhances the riddle of the eyes. Perhaps when they were first painted, when the valley was young and there was a settlement instead of a sprawling city, those eyes looked down on everyone, reaching into their homes, their fields, and into the passing phases of their lives like an insinuating presence. Even today it could be a reflection of one's own mood, or cloud shadows racing across the stupa, that make the half-closed, lotus-shaped eyes sometimes frown, blaze with anger, enquire, or smile.

Pressing upon the stupa and separated from it by a paved perambulatory, is a circular wall of houses in which those connected with the stupa, pilgrims, traders and craftsmen, live. On their ground floors are tourist shops filled with instantly attractive trinkets and curios and presided over by Nepalese or Tibetan shopkeepers endlessly jovial with bargaining on their brains.

A plump Tibetan lady who years ago made me her brother, sews and embroiders Tibetan boots. A man who used to call me Apala, or father, before he married and had four children, presides over a modern shop with wall-to-wall showcases and cupboards. Once he displayed his wares jumbled together in a dark cave of a room. The old houses with their thatched or small tiled roofs are giving way to modern concrete, a great sadness since the atmosphere of the place is changing with each new building.

Beyond the circle of shops, which contain a Buddhist chapel and a Buddhist monastery, there grows a town of monasteries, chapels, houses, lodges, shops, and chang houses which sell local liquour. Some of the monasteries, all in the Tibetan architectural styles are grandly enormous, but none impose upon the stupa. It soars above them all.

I can remember a time when Boudhanath was a single jewel in the lotus of its encircling houses, with not an irreverence of concrete anywhere; when a florid whitewashed gateway spanned a narrow entrance so no disturbing vehicles could intrude. There was only one monastery then, rather a chapel-beside-the-home of the Chini Lama, a rotund jovial man whose first concession to the modern world was giving audience from under a golf umbrella. It was he who supervised the ritual bathing of the stupa and the offering of votive flags that hang in strings from the high finial to the surrounding wall like the spokes of a great wheel.

Then in 1959 came the Tibetan refugees and with them a reincarnate lama known as the Mongolian lama who began to set up a fine monastery, a chant away from the Chini Lama. Both claimed to represent the Dalai Lama and both suggested, not always discreetly, that the other was a lesser lama. Time has changed all that. The Chini Lama is now over ninety years old, and reincarnates of every Tibetan Buddhist sect have, or are, raising monasteries.

Undoubtedly, the stupa is very old: some believe, older than the Buddha himself, others that in the heart of the stupa are enshrined relics of the Buddha brought from India by his beloved disciple Ananda. Perhaps the Emperor Ashoka who is believed to have visited the valley in the footsteps of his master, added to a stupa already there.

Over the centuries Boudhanath has been embellished, fallen into disrepair, and again added to by saints and kings. One of the last well-known donors to the stupa was the first maharaja prime minister, Jung Bahadur, who had a high prayer-wall built around the stupa where hundreds of copper prayer wheels are still turned by the pious.

Whatever its origin, whoever built it, there is a tranquillity, an other-wordly beauty about Boudhanath that no one fails to notice. Some claim cosmic forces or psychic vibrations, other the centuries of faith built into the stupa. Whatever, there is a wondrous sense of peace, contentment and well-being that surrounds the stupa.

The voice of legend requires a hearing. An early king of Kathmandu constructed a pool near his palace but no water poured from the three stone fountains carved with dragon heads. Deeply perplexed, the king consulted his oracles who advised that a man possessed of the thirty-two virtues should be sacrificed at the spot. So the king summoned his son and commanded him to go to the spring at dawn and sever the head of a shrouded person he would find sleeping there. Dutifully the son carried out the king's request, and even as water gushed from the fountains, he realised he had slain his father.

So great was his grief that he left the court and sought seclusion as an ascetic in a distant temple, but his penance alone was not enough to relieve the drought and plagues that befell his kingdom. When it seemed the whole valley was doomed, the prince had a vision in which the goddess Bajra

Yogini told him to build a great shrine to the Buddha where a white bird would settle.

So severe was the drought that there was no water with which to mix the clay and sand. So for twelve long years white sheets were spread upon the ground each night to be saturated with dew. When wrung out, the sheets provided the necessary water and so was built the stupa of a million dewdrops.

Peace and plenty returned to the land.

The Mystery of the Black Bhairab

 One of the piquant qualities of the great black Bhairab in Kathmandu's Durbar Square, is that no one knows where it originally came from, the temple or even the town in which it stood, who the craftsmen were or to which age they belonged.

It was found lying face down near a royal forest where a Malla king was constructing a garden. To many it was miraculous, as all statues that 'rise from the earth' or 'fall from the heavens' are. The other great stone statue that was similarly 'found,' is the image of Buddhanilkanth, the sleeping Vishnu, which belongs to the fourth or fifth century AD.

The black Bhairab is more crudely carved, but its power matches the overwhelming might of its subject, a six-armed god standing triumphantly upon a demon, cloaked in human skins and garlanded with human heads. He wears an ornate golden headdress, snakes writhe from his ears instead of earrings and coil about his neck, and in his hands holds an upraised sword, a *chakra*, a trident, severed heads and a bowl so reddened with vermilion it might contain blood. Carved flames dance about the tableau.

Purists would have the statue cleaned of its colour but here it is unnecessary, the black figure hung with red and yellow and white against a raw cobalt sky in which are set a vermilion and yellow sun and moon with human faces, projects a

stunning force no ordinary stone could achieve. There is
sacrificial blood on the figure which appears necessary for so
powerfully primitive a god who instils majesty with fear and
protects with terror.

From dawn till late evening there are worshippers at the
spot, mostly women wrapped in shawls and making offerings
of rice, vermilion, incense and oil lamps and flowers.

How so massive a statue was brought to where it now
stands in the old palace square, miles apart from where it was
discovered, is yet another riddle that attaches to the image.

When it was raised in its present position, guarded by two stone lions and attended by a panel of *ashtamatrikas*, it took on a new quality.

People accused of cheating or lying were brought before the Bhairab to swear their innocence. If they lied, they would surely die of a mysterious bleeding. Modern justice has discontinued the practice, but it is possible that in dark ceremonies no passers-by see, oaths are still taken before the frightening presence.

Bhairab represents the awesome, destructive forces of Shiva who, if properly propitiated, becomes the omnipotent guardian. As such he is venerated throughout Nepal, making him the most popular of all deities. His image is everywhere, often just a head because legend is filled with stories of how Bhairab was decapitated.

One tells how Bhairab came from Kashi, Benares, in India, to visit the New Year festivals in the guise of a man. People soon grew suspicious of a tall, handsome stranger in their midst and informed their priests. Using tantric rites the priests soon discovered that the stranger was indeed Bhairab, so they plotted to bind him with spells and keep him in the valley. Bhairab, finding himself trapped, tried hurriedly to sink into the earth and escape, but as he disappeared the people cut off his head, which they enshrined and have worshipped ever since.

Perhaps the children who told me that the great black Bhairab had come from heaven were right. Their reasoning might surprise scholars, for they had him so gorged on the wicked and on demons that he could no longer fly. Why did he not fly away again when he was empty? Because the people of Kathmandu keep him happy, they said, and there is, if you look long enough at that wide-eyed, grimacing face, a scarlet smile of pleasure.

The Forgotten Shrine of the Sikhs

Books on Kathmandu are silent about the shrine. It is not on the tourist map. No coaches park below the small forested hill by the river on the road to Balaju. The temple is left to bird song and the occasional visitor who either knows it is there or by chance comes upon the small weathered sign which says 'Guru Nanak Math'.

An arching stairway leads through trees and bamboo to the small building which from the outside looks like a Nepalese farmhouse. I find the climb up the stairs refreshing even though a bit breathless. The city, which now encroaches on the fields about the hill, is screened by greenery and might not exist. The busy sound of traffic trails further and further behind. Through windows in the trees can be seen the river and a high mountain. A small grassy clearing just before the house is just the kind of place a weary traveller would have welcomed. Cool. Quiet. Undisturbed.

The doorway to the lime-washed house is plastered with ochre earth. The black painted door is small in the way of old Nepal, so one stoops to enter. An old man, asleep on the clean, earthen floor sits up and smiles a welcome. His dog, curled up beside him, takes no notice. I beg his pardon. Perhaps I've made a mistake. I'm looking for the Guru Nanak Math.

He leads me barefooted across a freshly plastered courtyard

at the centre of which is a small shrine with a *tulsi* plant growing out of the top. It is difficult to make out the deities in the small niches but he agrees, as I think aloud, that they are Vishnu, Shiva and Parvati, Hanuman and Pashupatinath.

In a verandah are steep stairs which we climb to enter into a small dark room. At the centre, under a canopy, is an altar draped in red. Here, says my companion, reposes the Granth Sahib, written by Guru Nanak himself in letters of gold. I ask him to repeat what he said because if he is correct, then this almost forgotten shrine in a land not normally associated with the saint, possesses a rare and unique relic.

Strangely, the priest who is Nepalese, wears none of the symbols of Sikhism; turban, *kada, kirpan* or *kanga*. However, his greying hair is unshorn and, for a Nepalese, he sports a fair beard. I learn, with undisguised excitement, that he belongs to the earliest unreformed order of Sikhs who are often unrecognisable from Vaishnavite Hindus. At Pashupatinath, I would have taken him for a sadhu.

He whispered me out of the courtyard into a small garden wild with shrubs and flowers. Under a large peepal tree he pointed out a stone slab on which were carved two feet, laid with roses. 'The guru's,' he said. 'It is at this spot that Guru Nanak sat in meditation. In that little shrine behind you, are buried the ashes of a Nepalese king.'

We sat together on mossy steps leading up to the shrine, a strong scent of jasmine in the air and two *bulbuls* pecking about the carved feet. And there he told me the story of the temple of the golden book and the shrine against which we sat.

It seems a Malla king of the early sixteenth century — the priest did not know his name — suffered a disturbed mind. His brothers, alarmed by his behaviour, banished him to India. Roaming forlornly through the holy city of Benares he came upon the saint Guru Nanak and begged him to cure his affliction. After many visits and much beseeching, the guru advised the king to return to his kingdom where his health would be restored.

Miraculously, the saint preceded the king to Kathmandu for there he was, meditating under a peepal tree on a hill beside the river. The king visited him at once, begging the guru to return with him to the palace. Guru Nanak refused to do so, saying that in this serene spot he had all he wanted. So the king had a temple built for his guru and a small shrine for himself where he often came to meditate. When the king died, some of his ashes were buried in the shrine according to his last wishes.

A later king, Rana Bahadur Shah, also of unsound mind, is said to have found solace at the Guru Nanak Math. He gifted considerable land to the temple so it might never want for support.

Perhaps the records have long since perished because slowly the gurudwara lands have been encroached upon until only the hill remains. It would be a tragedy if modern hungers consume the trees and push concrete within reach of the peaceful old building.

When I went back to sketch the garden and the temple, I was met by another old priest. I asked him if I might see the guru's footprints. 'Ah yes,' he said 'they are the Guru Nanak's feet, but they are also Vishnu's. They are both the same.'

And who, I asked, wrote the golden book enshrined in the temple. 'Sri Chand, the guru's son,' he said. Was it not Guru Nanak?

By then the guru had gone to Tibet, he said. 'But it is all the same. Our gods are our gods.'

Obviously the lovely, lonely Guru Nanak Math is in need of a Sikh scholar to unravel its truths and its legends. Until then it will remain a half-forgotten temple on a wooded hill threatened by the brick and concrete advances of Kathmandu.

The Gate of the Vermilion god

 The palace is centuries old and in all probability it stands on older foundations. Built partly by the Malla kings, it was added to by the Gurkha monarch Prithvi Narayan Shah when he over ran the valley of Kathmandu in 1768. The autocratic Ranas who held sway for 104 years added a touch of Kathmandu colonial. The present king, Birendra Bir Bikram Shah Dev, who resides in a modern palace a couple of miles away, has had the ancient buildings painstakingly restored rather than added to.

Partly open to the public, the old Durbar is a gem set in the centre of the city. There are at least ten courtyards or *chowks,* embellished with polished brick and exquisitely carved wood, gilded metal intricately fashioned, white plaster tracery on white plaster, carved stone, painted wood, and a brilliance of statuary and temples.

There is but one common gateway to all this magnificence — a golden doorway known as the Hanuman Dhoka. It takes its name from the kneeling figure of Hanuman that guards the gate, a statue so covered with years of votive dress and vermilion that it has lost its shape.

A mouth silently snarls in the scarlet, featureless face. Scarlet robes drape its powerful figure. A tinsel-edged scarlet cloth covers its head and eyes. Tourist guides will tell you that

his eyes are veiled to prevent him from seeing the erotic carvings on the nearby Jagganath temple. He is shielded by a painted Nepalese umbrella that is changed once a year. And attended by youths who climb like monkeys onto the high pedestal to offer votive offerings and give prasad in return.

Hanuman was greatly regarded by the Mallas who claimed descent from Ram Chandra. His image is seen in all the old palaces of the valley and countless are his shrines. The vermilion Hanuman at the old Kathmandu palace gate was erected at the command of King Pratap Malla in 1672. At that time, the palace gateway was probably made of heavy wood and iron. In 1810 the reigning Gurkha king decided upon the extravagance of a golden gate. There was one of exceptional beauty in the royal palace at Bhatgaon and great was the rivalry between these cities.

Unfortunately, the basic copper from which the gate was fashioned was obtained by melting down plates inscribed with the history of Kathmandu, and so were lost invaluable records

The Gate of the Vermilion god / **21**

of earlier rulers and their times. But then history is full of such careless excesses. Looking at the handsome gate today one is just happy it is there. Though he didn't know it at the time, the king was providing a tourist attraction that sets thousands of cameras clicking today.

As I sat sketching, an American matron insisted her husband take yet another shot of the gate, this time without her. When he hesitated, she said, 'Go on honey, it's real gold.' Well, he might have wished the same of her.

Beside the awesome Hanuman, the gate is guarded by Shiva and Shakti riding lions; painted stone statues that predate the vermilion monkey god. Above the golden doorway and a panel of painted deities are three groups of figures. One is of Krishna and two *gopinis*. Another is probably of King Pratap Malla and his queen, and the third is thought to represent a scene from the Mahabharat.

Supplementing all these divine forces are two Gurkha guards, one dressed in the ancient black and white uniform of Prithvi Narayan's soldiers, armed with a musket, long bayonet fixed, that makes it taller than the man, and the other in modern army green, carrying a cane. The black uniformed troops attend every important festival, carrying standards and flags as old as the history of the Gurkhas and marching to the music of flutes and drums.

A small fee gets one through the gate into the palace. Rather, into the Nasal Chowk, the largest courtyard in the sprawl of royal buildings. Legend has it that King Pratap Malla, a poet and dancer of renown, once dressed and danced publicly as Narsingh, which so infuriated the god he cursed the king to dance forever. The king's passionate pleading and his promise to have a statue worthy of the god made and installed at the spot lifted the curse. Just inside the gate is a striking black marble image of Narsingh decorated with gold and silver: the king's penance.

It is in the Nasal Chowk, looked down upon by many-splendoured towers and temple spires, that the Shah kings are crowned. Distinguished visitors crowd three sides of the courtyard, a military honour guards the fourth. According to ancient Vedic rites and at the exact moment considered most auspicious the king is crowned, his queen by his side. They then sit on a golden throne, under a canopy of raised serpent heads, and the royal couple accept the homage of all present.

The king and queen arrive through the Hanuman Dhoka dressed in simple homespun and leave in silks and brocades, magnificently crowned and bejewelled. Outside, waits the royal tusker, richly caparisoned, which leads a procession of howdah elephants through the main streets of Kathmandu.

Kings, queens, nobles, courtiers, conspirators, assassins, plenipotentiaries, invaders, soothsayers, priests; the gate of the monkey god has seen them all. And now it is the turn of the tourists. Perhaps King Pratap Malla foresaw their coming when he had erected, near the gate, a slab of stone engraved in several languages, a word in English, a couple in French. Obviously no one told him about Spaniards, Japanese and Russians.

Where Serpents Breathe Fire

 Described in an early guide book as 'Bhim Sen's greatest erection,' a nine-storied minaret with an imposing gilded finial is Kathmandu's most prominent landmark. It was built in 1832 by one of Nepal's greatest soldier statesman, Bhim Sen Thapa, who virtually ruled Nepal as prime minister, when he was shamefully killed by his enemies at court, who had much to revenge. The British resident in Nepal, Brian Hodgson, wrote to the governor general in India, Lord Moira, 'thus has perished the great and able statesman who for more than thirty years had ruled this kingdom with more than regal sway.'

The tower apparently was built to serve as a lookout post and from which buglers sounded alarms. But I wonder if Bhim Sen Thapa, who commanded his Nepalese forces most valiantly against those of Sir David Ochterlony in the 1814-16 Gurkha Wars, wasn't simply building a triumphal folly on Kathmandu's parade ground, Tundikhel, just as a similar minaret was erected on Calcutta's Maidan in honour of Sir Ochterlony.

One of Bhim Sen's illustrious descendants, the first Rana prime minister Jung Bahadur, is believed to have ridden his horse up the narrow steps of the tower and jumped from the top. The horse died but Jung Bahadur survived. An old Nepalese professor friend of mine assured me that Jung Bahadur used an umbrella.

Almost immediately below Bhim Sen's tower which is surrounded by a pseudo-Gothic screen, is an ancient sunken public bath fed by clear water from carved fountains. The place is always crowded. Where the abundant water comes from or where it goes is unknown; my professor insisted it came from 'the holy mountains.' This is one of Kathmandu's few public springs still in use. All over the valley, beautifully carved stone and gilded fountains are dry because, apparently, the underground water level has dropped.

My sketch of the minar, known as the Bhim Sen Stumbha

or Dharara, shows a temple to the god Mahadeva which Bhim Sen apparently had built. As I sketched the Muslim inspired dome, over which writhe four golden and plumed serpents, a small boy told me how once he and his mother came at dawn to wash in a nearby tank. Suddenly, bright blue flames flared from the serpents' mouths, causing them to run for their lives. 'Several people have seen the fires,' he said.

In the three years since I first sketched the temple, it has grown a fair forest below its dome and modern construction has encroached to within feet of it. Lorries park among adoring images of Hanuman and Bhairab. Where a wing of Bhim Sen's palace once stood are now piles of rubble. It is rumoured that a new five-star hotel, named after a famous British prime minister, will one day occupy the spot. What is left of the palace, once known as Bagh Mahal, and later Hari Bhavan, is occupied by an Indian mission. Interestingly, the name Bagh Mahal commemorates the time when cages of tigers stood by the gates to the palace.

I was once shown around the now demolished wing of the palace by a young man who claimed to be a member of the occupying family. We entered a small gate, walked through a crumbling courtyard and groped our way down a maze of narrow, low passageways that led to a gallery overlooking what had once been a large lily pond surrounded by rose gardens. Close to where we stood, the gallery descended in a brief stairway leading to a closed door. 'This is where they brought the prisoners,' explained my host, 'and behind there is where they were executed.'

I never discovered who the prisoners were or why they were executed because the young man with a distinct touch of the morbid had other horrors to unfold. 'Up there,' he said, pointing to a window in a tower, 'was where Bhim Sen was imprisoned and driven to suicide. His tormentors told him that his wife was being made to walk the streets of Kathmandu, stark naked. In great anguish, he broke a window pane and slashed his wrists.' History says he used a *khukri* conveniently left in the room by his guards.

Plunging me into another, older courtyard which was built about a shrine, my guide told me how an unidentified prince had himself shut in the temple to meditate. Before the heavy doors were closed behind him the prince cautioned his wife that he was not to be disturbed for a certain number of days and not at all if she found proof of his having achieved eternal bliss. When she returned at the stipulated time there was no answer to her calls, but from under the door was a trickle of blood. When the door was opened, the horrified Rani and her retinue found only the idol wet with blood. This small courtyard has been left standing and because of its sanctity will probably be spared.

When all else is swept away, one hopes the handsome minaret will remain as a monument to a great, if ruthlessly ambitious man.

Processions for a Grieving Queen

A short while ago in Kathmandu, just after the first full August moon, the valley celebrated Gai Jatra, the festival of sacred cows. Families bereaved during the past year honour the souls of their dead by taking out processions along routes dictated by history. In this colourful way they appease Yama Raj, the god of death, and ensure that a friendly cow will guide the souls of their dear departed through the dangers of the underworld by letting them cling to its tail. If rituals are correctly followed and good deeds done on Gai Jatra day, the cow will be even more than a useful guide. It will help push open the gates of Yama's kingdom.

In Kathmandu, the processions comprise real cows, children dressed to represent cows and holy men. Also, the family priest. Inevitably they are joined by crowds of others so that procession joins procession to form a vivid human stream flowing through streets and squares to the sound of drums and flutes and chanting. The boys are gorgeously costumed in the brightest silks and brocades, *zari*-gold, dominating reds and shocking pinks, their faces painted, eyes enlarged with kajal, their head dresses bouquets of flowers surrounding paper cow masks. Horns are bamboo hung with painted pennants. Behind them hang tails of white cloth. Usually the smallest boy is dressed as a yogi in white and saffron, liberally powdered to suggest ashes.

The more affluent walk under ceremonial umbrellas, preceded by bands. Here and there a small boy succumbs to the temptation of fruit stalls and ice cream carts, but only briefly. The processions must begin and end at times declared auspicious. So, as suddenly as the city is filled with their colour and music, so it is drained of it. Who laid down the procession route and when may not be remembered, but there is one spot that all must pass — an ivory, gold and wooden window of the old palace. For here, in the eighteenth century, King Pratap Malla and his queen sat to watch the passing processions.

Tradition has it that the queen was inconsolable at the death of their son. Nothing, it seemed, could dispel her grief.

Processions for a Grieving Queen / **29**

The king had a procession of cows sent out in the boy's memory, and when that failed to comfort the queen, he ordered that every family bereaved that year should do the same. In this way she would know she was not alone in her grief. Those who had no cows sent their children out instead. The family priest gave a correct gravity to the occasion, the music lightened its sadness. The queen remained wrapped in her sorrow.

So the king announced a reward to any of his subjects who could bring joy to his wife, and at the same time exonerated them from any offence their efforts might cause. His fun-loving people appeared below the palace window in droves, preposterously dressed and lampooning everything from social injustice to questionable behaviour in high places. The queen was delighted. She laughed for the first time in months, so the king immediately ordained that similar parades be made part of Gai Jatra forever more.

The fun and frolic persist to this day. Extraordinarily dressed people appear on the streets. Small groups of people delight the crowds with satirical plays. Everyone and everybody with the exception of the royal family comes in for good natured ridicule. Special newspapers are printed that make the wildest claims and give the kind of news everyone dreams of reading.

Patan, the city of the artist, celebrates with gaily dressed children in noisy processions, for it is believed that noise frightens away evil spirits and the souls of those who refuse to leave the living world. Girls in flowing dresses and wreaths in their hair move in slow procession before the old royal palace, pausing every now and again under shading ceremonial umbrellas.

In old Bhaktapur, the 'cows' are towering constructions of bamboo wrapped in sarees, surmounted by brightly coloured cow masks, large cloth-bound horns, yak hair, flowers, buntings and incongruous parasols. Photographs of the dead are usually displayed. Musicians and troupes of dancers prance endlessly in front of each tableau, until they all meet in a square towered over by temples and joined there by a Bhairab made of straw. One looks in wonder not just at the present festivities but into a past of primitive beauty. Somehow the mystery and tragedy of dying is made that bit easier by these processions of remembrance. Like a queen of old, one laughs at one's grief.

A Goddess from Calcutta?

 The old trade route from Tibet to India cuts diagonally through Kathmandu. More truthfully, Kathmandu grew about the trade route now called Asan. At one end is a tank, many elephants deep, constructed by a king. At the other is the glorious complex of the old royal palace, teeming with history, temples and statuary. Every here and there the narrow street, if it can be called such, widens into a square dominated by temples. One of the most beautiful temples is the one dedicated to Annapurna.

At first sight, particularly if the sun is right, the temple appears to be made from solid gold. Its three pagoda roofs are heavily gilded, as are its finial, its richly fashioned doorway, the decorative birds, the metal frills, the divine faces on the ribbed roofs and the ornate torana over the door. Obviously, much expense and devoted labour was lavished on its construction. Instead of an image, there is a silver *purnakalash*, wound around by a silver serpent and draped with a silver scarf. Gilded lions guard the entrance.

Temple records are dated 1839 and show that the building required renovation by the end of the nineteenth century. Here tradition takes over. Known as Asan Maju Ajima, the grandmother goddess of Asan, Annapurna is the goddess of plenty. Once dwelling in either Benares or Calcutta, she grew

restless for the mountains and begged to be brought to Kathmandu. There she was installed under a tree, the stump of which can still be seen in the temple. She faces west and perhaps in those distant, uncrowded times no buildings or pollution obstructed her view of the magnificent mountains that bear her name.

Many years ago in Calcutta I sketched an ancient temple to Annapurna, daughter of the Himalayas, which stood crumbling beside the Diamond Harbour Road. If I remember rightly, the property belonged to the Roy Choudhury family of Barisa. Mr Pratap Roy Choudhury spoke of the times when much of what is now Calcutta belonged to his ancestors. They had leased the villages of Sutanuti, Govindapur and Kalikata to Job *Charnok* and had helped to build the Kalighat temple.

There was no image in the picturesque ruin of the temple. A banyan tree grew luxuriantly out of the pillared building, holding it together rather than destroying it. Could this have been where Asan's goddess Annapurna once dwelt and longed for the hills? A pleasing thought even if unsubstantiated by fact.

Today, Asan is a bustling square, clamourous with people, street vendors, rickshaws, cars that can hardly budge, cows and even the occasional elephant. Devotees pause before Annapurna or perambulate around the temple, making offerings and receiving *prasad* in return. Perhaps in acknowledgement of the goddess of plenty, the government sets up a supply shop in times of kerosene shortage almost under the golden roofs. People carrying tins and plastic containers queue snake-like about the temple. Close by are shops selling Nepalese candles that ease periodic power cuts.

Modern houses of no particular architectural style or beauty crowd behind the gilded temple. The goddess herself gazes across the square to a gilded Ganesh temple imprisoned in thoughtless electric pylons. Will she grow restless again for freedom? I doubt it. There can be no more fascinating a square anywhere as Asan. Even for a goddess.

When a Goddess Played Dice

 The temple is the most majestic in all of Kathmandu. Its legends are the most romantic. When it was built in 1576, at the command of a king, it was required to be seen from the old city of Bhaktapur, some ten miles away, from where the resident goddess was brought. No other building was permitted to rise higher than its gilded roofs and golden finial. To attain its imposing height, it was raised on several receding brick plinths. The plinths alone would rival an Aztec temple and the mind boggles to think of how they were made, of how many people laboured to construct them, of the enormity of faith or discipline that inspired the builders.

Several small pagoda-style temples, housing the guardians of the eight directions and the Panchayan gods, are set symmetrically upon the plinths. They supplement, rather than detract from the soaring magnificence of the temple itself. A paved courtyard away is the old palace, its roofs pierced by many fine temple spires and pavilions, but the temple of Teleju surpasses them all as if proudly conscious that it enshrines the royal goddess.

Teleju Bhawani is a goddess from South India who well may feel far from home were it not for the great devotion lavished on her here. She was brought to Nepal in the early fourteenth century by Harisingha Deva, a Karnatak king who

ruled over the small kingdom of Simroanghar in the foothills of present-day Nepal. When Ghiyas-ud-din Tughlak, who had marched on Bengal to suppress a rebellion, was returning triumphantly home to Delhi, he laid seige to Simroanghar. The royal family, the court and presumably the defeated army, fled northwards into Nepal. Here historical opinion is divided. Either the Malla king, then resident in Bhaktapur, fled before this unintended invasion and abandoned his kingdom to Harisingha Deva, who established a Karnatak dynasty in the Kathmandu valley; or Harisingha Deva was hospitably received as a royal refugee by the Malla king and given the freedom of the valley for as long as he cared to stay. His influence on the political and cultural scene was nevertheless great. It is believed by many to this day that the highly talented people of the Kathmandu valley, the Newars, derived their name from the Nayas who accompanied the Karnatak king, and remained to intermarry with the local people. One of the greatest Malla kings was of mixed Malla and Karnatak descent.

As soon as Ghiyas-ud-din Tughlak tired of besieging Simroanghar and marched away, King Harisingha Deva returned home. He left behind him his son, who was to rule the valley, several members of his court, and the precious gift of Teleju Bhawani. The goddess came to be greatly venerated by the kings of Nepal. The magnificent Teleju temple was built to enshrine her and here only royalty may worship except at Dussehra when the public is permitted to enter, to pray and make sacrifices.

Legend takes over. Some two hundred years ago a young Newari girl found wandering outside the palace claimed to be possessed by the spirit of Teleju Bhawani. When the news was brought to him, the king, thinking her to be an evil imposter, had her banished from the kingdom. Within hours, one of his queens suffered not only convulsions but delusions that she too was possessed by the spirit of the goddess. The worried king had a search made for the girl and finding her declared her to be the Living Goddess Kumari. The queen was immediately cured. A more colourful story has Jaya Prakash Malla, the very same king, playing dice with the goddess Teleju, who appeared to him as a beautiful mortal after his devotions. While they played, she advised him on affairs of state, a happy and helpful situation that would have continued had not the king one night looked lustfully upon the goddess. In great wrath she announced she would never come to him again. Worse, she predicted that both the end of his reign and the fall of his dynasty were at hand. When the king begged humbly for forgiveness, the goddess made a strange concession. The king was to select a virgin child from a Newari caste, proclaim her the Living Goddess Kumari, and worship her, for in this child she herself would manifest.

A third, more human story, has the goddess Teleju playing dice with King Jaya Prakash Malla as before, but herself succumbing to a very ungodly failing. One of the queens, growing suspicious of her husband's nightly disappearances followed him to his rendezvous where the goddess saw her peeping from behind a curtain. Mistaking the queen's curiosity for a betrayal of the king's vow never to tell anyone of their meeting, the goddess immediately vanished. Appearing to him in a dream that night she informed the king that she would never return, but he would find her if he searched, in the guise of a virgin child of the Sakya class.

Whatever the legend, the consequence is the same. A desolate and repentent king at once ordered a search for a suitable child. When she was discovered with the help of his advisers and priests, King Jaya Prakash Malla had a fine dwelling built for her close to his place and within sight of the temple to Teleju.

There she was installed with great ceremony and jubilation and the king instituted a yearly jatra in her honour. Perhaps, in the midst of all this joyful activity he forgot something very important. The goddess Teleju Bhawani's prophecy; the loss of his kingdom and the fall of his dynasty.

The House of the Living Goddess

How to build a house for a goddess? What magnificence can match a deity's supreme importance? What provisions to make? What skills to employ? Temples, mosques and churches the world over have faced similar problems, but they are only houses of prayer. In Kathmandu, when a king ordered a fitting abode built for a Living Goddess, his architects, mere mortals themselves, designed a house built about a courtyard with carved windows of outstanding beauty. It faces onto Durbar Square, a road's breadth from the old royal palace, and looking out onto temples and platforms on which kings once sat to give royal audience.

The entrance to the building is guarded by large stone lions. The window at which the Kumari can sometimes be seen and from where, in olden times, she gave *darshan,* is two stories above, exquisitely carved and gilded. Several other windows, adorned with deities, garudas, strange water monsters and dancing peacocks adorn the plain white façade. A triple finial rides the tiled roof like a golden boat in full sail.

Carved windows and verandahs open onto the courtyard. Nowadays the Kumari makes obliging appearances at one of these inner windows for crowding tourists. A notice near the stairs leading to the top floors warns — 'For Hindus Only'— who are permitted to enter an audience chamber where they may receive *tikka* from the Living Goddess herself. Here,

during the Indra *Jatra*, which coincides with the Kumari Jatra in early September, the king comes to receive *tikka* from the Kumari and obtain from her the right to rule another year. In exchange he presents her with a golden coin and touches his forehead to her feet.

Many are the stories current in Kathmandu of how the Kumari has failed, for one reason or the other, to bless a suppliant king, and how tragedy has resulted. There is the tale of a Rana maharaja who, failing to receive the Kumari's blessing, was soon after exiled by his avaricious brothers. Another describes how a *vaid* treating the Kumari for some minor ailment, somehow offended her. He no longer lives to tell the tale. Such an aura of mysticism understandably attaches itself to a child of such singular importance.

40 / *In the Kingdom of the Gods*

Though worshipped and revered as a Hindu goddess, the Kumari is selected from the Newari caste of Sakya goldsmiths, who are Buddhists. She must have the thirty-two virtues, among which are an unblemished body, the voice of a bird, the neck of a duck. She must never cry or show fear, nor bleed at puberty or as a result of any of the small injuries that normal children experience. Her horoscope must match that of the king in every detail.

This means that no Kumari reigns for more than a few years, for at the first sign of approaching menstruation she is relieved of her high status and retired into the world from which she came, rich but no doubt transformed and unsettled by her extraordinary experience. Free to marry she seldom finds a husband because tradition decrees death to any man who ends her virginity. However, there now exists the precedent of a married Kumari, so the future may be happier for these briefly privileged girls.

The tantric rites surrounding the selection of a Kumari are so well guarded that few know really what passes. The child is only three or four years old when discovered, much too young to have the capacity to put on an act taught by her parents. One of her many required virtues is to have an emotional control that would be the envy of most adults. To test her courage, for instance, it is said that the child must spend a night in a temple surrounded by the severed heads of sacrificed animals. Grotesquely masked men leap and scream about her. Amazingly, she emerges from her ordeal without a trace of fear.

The festival of Indra, the Lord of the Heaven, who once visited the Kathmandu valley in the guise of a handsome mortal, and Kumari, the Living Goddess, blend together in early September. All Kathmandu gathers from earliest dawn to watch the procession of *raths,* crowding nearby temple plinths, windows, balconies and roofs. The king, himself considered a reincarnation of Vishnu, his ministers, officials, and foreign dignitaries, appear on a balcony of the old palace, from where the king showers coins upon the Kumari and her attendants, two virgin boys, who represent Bhairab and Ganesh. Each is enthroned in a *rath* of his own. A goat is sacrificed in front of the Kumari's chariot, muskets fire a startling volley and the procession moves, the young Living Goddess dressed in gold and fine silks, bejewelled and exotically painted, sitting serenely among her attendants. Masked dancers leap and brandish swords. Colourfully dressed tantric Buddhist priests chant mantras. The crowds press forward to take a turn on the chariot ropes.

Small child that she is, the Kumari rides out the clamour and excitement of her jatra with a face remarkably composed. Sometimes, just sometimes, there is the trace of excitement that any child would feel. Could it be that she remembers a similar jatra two centuries ago, when the goddess Teleju's dire prophecy came true? As the people of Kathmandu celebrated the festival with great joy and excessive drinking, the Gurkha King Prithvi Narayan Shah attacked and easily overcame the city. The Malla king Jaya Prakash fled, his dynasty at an end. The Gurkha king ordered the festival to continue. It is said he himself lent a hand to pull the Kumari's *rath*.

The Hill of the Flaming Lotus

Many many legends ago, the valley of Kathmandu was turquoise like, so beautiful that sages who came to meditate along its shore considered it sacred. Upon its waters rested a single lotus from which rose a flame as colourful as a rainbow. In time it was called Swayambhu, the self-born, self-existent one. Among those who heard of its divine reputation was the great Mongolian saint Manjushri, who came to pay homage. When he saw the lotus for himself, so great was his desire to approach it that he cut the valley wall with his flaming sword of wisdom to allow the water to drain away. The lotus settled on a low hill and there Manjushri worshipped and caused a shrine to be built. As people settled in the new valley, the city they built was called Manjupatan.

A combination of legend and history places the origin of the great stupa of Swayambhunath about two thousand years ago. While repudiating divine intervention, geologists support the belief that the Kathmandu valley was once under water. Swayambhunath hill was probably an island, which in a way it is today, a forested island in emerald fields which attracts pious individuals and religious institutions as certainly as it did the sages of old.

Several Tibetan monasteries have begun to ring the hill and even climb it. An adjoining hill is covered with buildings housing such diverse people as neohippies, Tibetan refugees, Buddhist nuns, the first Western rinpoche, artists and Tibetologists. One of the nuns, who claims to have lived centuries ago when the reigning Malla king was so impressed by meeting her that he gifted her land and money for a monastery, tells fortunes and unhexes the hexed. I've taken a problem to her. She's quite impressive.

Leading to the top of the hill are a flight of ancient steps and in recent years, a motorable road that stops reverently short of the summit. To take the 365 steps is not only meritorious but rewarding as well, for it climbs through trees and piled rock, past huge painted images of the Buddha and the traditional vehicle of the gods, a horse, an elephant, a peacock, a garuda, a lion. There are also the imprints of Manjushri's feet in stone. And hoardes of monkeys which have given Swayambhunath stupa the popular tourist name, 'monkey temple'. A slightly irreverent legend accounts for them also. When Manjushri had his hair cut on the hill, every hair became a tree and the lice became monkeys. A completely serious and learned survey by a foreign agency has concluded that the number of monkeys always remain the same.

Where the steps grow suddenly steep below the summit, iron hand rails have been thoughtfully provided, that help the failing pilgrim only when children and monkeys permit. It's a fairly shattering experience the first time around to find monkeys sliding towards one at vast speed, chattering happily to themselves as they pass by. The children merely imitate them. I've always wished one could slide rapidly upward, for legend again promises nirvana and all the bliss in it to those who can climb the 365 stairs in a single breath.

At the foot of the stairs are three old and enormous statues of Gautama Buddha in meditation. Old people make obeisance as they pass, touching their foreheads to the

crumbling pedestals. The young climb the statues happily in play or to pose for tourist cameras. The benign expressions never change. The huge hands remain at rest. If their meditation permits, what amazing sights they must have seen!

Every twelve years in a field nearby, the reigning king of Nepal comes as Vishnu incarnate, and an aspect of Buddha, to receive the homage of hundreds of gilded Buddha statues brought from all over the valley. Countless Hindus and Buddhists climb the hill to worship, for Swayambhunath is sacred to them both. As I sat to sketch, procession after procession, each led by a band of flutes, pipes and drums, descended the hill, marking the last day of the holy Buddhist month of Gunla.

Now a colourful Tibetan style gateway stands at the entrance to the stairs and a wall of prayer wheels promises to circumscribe the hill. Not far away is a small new monastery that enshrines some miraculous images. Long ago in Tibet,

The Hill of the Flaming Lotus / **45**

when an agnostic king tried to stamp out Buddhism, he came to the original monastery and declared to the assembled monks that if their deities were truly divine they would feel the cut of his sword. As he slashed at images about him they miraculously cried out in pain. Brought to Nepal in 1959, they remain happily mute.

It is possible to see Swayambhunath hill from every corner of the Kathmandu valley. There are magic moments when from a cloudy sky that shadows the entire landscape, a shaft of light illuminates the hill, its stupa and its golden spire. It is easy, then, to remember the ancient legend. The divine lotus floating on a lake. The mystic flame. The self-born, self-existent one — Swayambhu.

The Stupa Built by Time

 Upon a forested hill, like a cap of snow, is the great Buddhist stupa of Swayambhunath. Here the divine lotus that floated on a lake once filling the valley of Kathmandu, came to rest. Here the Saint Manjushri worshipped and built a small shrine. That is the legend.

No one really knows. A hilltop so prominent would have attracted sages and the religious from the time the valley was first peopled. Their offerings, perhaps merely stones or forest flowers, became a shrine, the shrine a stupa. It could be that Emperor Ashoka, who raised stupas in significant places about the valley, built one here, but there is no commemorative pillar, no inscription.

Learned Buddhist friends have assured me the stupa preceded the Buddha, but scholars are even hesitant to confirm the two thousand years that are usually claimed as its age. Two thousand years is a long time ago. Miracles were fairly commonplace. Gods walked the valley of Kathmandu. Could memory only from hearsay truly recall some natural phenomenon that caused the lake to empty itself so that an island became a hill and the hill a focus for worship and meditation? What does matter is that Swayambhu is perhaps Kathmandu's oldest monument. Also one of its most beautiful.

The great pearl of the stupa, whitewashed and streaked with the colours of worship, represents the creation. Upon it rests a square, gilded tower painted on four sides with the all-seeing eyes of the Buddha. Cobalt, white and red. Shaped like lotus petals. Gazing out across the valley with compassion. The Nepalese numeral one for a nose, symbolic of the true and only path. A third eye like a *tikka.* And above the tower, a soaring spire of thirteen golden rings, representing the steps of enlightenment, shaded by a gilded umbrella and a golden finial.

There is no plinth other than the hill itself. But around the stupa is an ornate metal fence onto which are set hundreds of prayer wheels. Into the stupa are embedded gilded shrines that house the Buddhas of the five directions (one is the centre), and their consorts. The entrances to these shrines are hung with gilded metal curtains that the devout draw aside to make offerings, and the monkeys, following closely after, prise open to steal. Strings of prayer flags hung between the top of the spire and surrounding buildings, flutter among the pigeons that wheel continuously about the stupa.

Some believe the flame that once burned at the heart of the lotus, still burns inside the stupa. That a great Buddhist tantric built the stupa as a cap over the flame. So romantic a belief has been dispelled by repairs made over the centuries, when the great wooden beam supporting the superstructure has had to be replaced.

More recently, when it seemed the whole of Swayambhunath hill was in danger of sliding into the valley, taking the stupa with it, a team of experts dug a great hole beside the stupa to determine the strength of its foundations. Some images dating back to the seventh and eighth centuries were found. Had this intriguing excavation reached under the stupa itself, the relics it contained would have incisively dated its origin. Or the experts would have been consumed by the divine flame. One confessed to having thought about it.

Over the centuries a clutter of monasteries, shrines, rest houses, images, dwellings and shops have lent an air of claustrophobia to the stupa. They crowd it, make it impossible to stand back far enough to see the elegantly proportioned shrine in all its glory, a dazzling crown on a hallowed hill. I've often wished them away, and some were recently demolished to prevent the possibility of further landslides, but then again they are the pulse of Swayambhunath, the life in its other-worldliness. From dawn to dusk they provide the movement and sounds of prayer, give significance to the importance of the shrine they crowd about. Some are almost as important as the stupa itself. Many have legends as colourful.

There is the golden roofed pagoda temple dedicated to Hariti Ajima, the grandmother goddess who protects children from diseases, particularly smallpox, and has been known to comfort more adult problems. She is a Hindu goddess seen by Buddhists to be a reincarnation of Buddha's mother Maya Devi, and so is worshipped by both religions. There is hardly a moment when elaborate *pujas* are not being performed before the intricately carved silver doors of Ajima's temple. A king of Nepal was once mad enough to have the temple demolished. A Rana general had it hastily rebuilt and richly adorned its gilded roofs which almost touch the bowl of the stupa.

Further away is the unimaginatively restored temple of Shantipur, which exudes a sense of dark history. It is whispered that there is a miraculous pool inside, that a cave reaches all the way to Tibet. Only the temple priest may enter to worship and feed the deities. The story goes that once, when the priest asked what the gods wished to eat they answered, 'that which walks behind you.' To his horror, he discovered his daughter had followed him to the temple, but the sacrifice had to be made. From that day young Nepalese children have worn bells.

Most interesting is the small temple to Saraswati, for Buddhists consider her to be the consort of Manjushri, and students of both faiths flock to her shrine to benefit from the wisdom of both deities, yet another example of how closely Hinduism and Buddhism coexist in Nepal.

To mark the 2,500th Buddha Jayanti celebrations held in Kathmandu, delegates from all the Buddhist world contributed towards a new monastery on Swayambhu hill. Its concrete is yet to mellow, but its lamp-lit interior may have been there since a Malla king and queen raised towering temples to their own glory on either side of Swayambhunath centuries ago. Its huge gilt image of the Buddha is impressive, its lamas delightfully hospitable. But what I remember most vividly is that a Tibetan reincarnate lama used to sit in an upstairs room writing music.

He was putting the poems of the Buddhist saint Milarepa to rock music for Western audiences.

The Golden Mask of the White Bhairab

 One of the most dramatic sights in Kathmandu, heightened by the fact that it is revealed only once a year and then only for a few days is the great golden mask of Seto Bhairab, in the Durbar Square. For those who remember J. Milton Hayes' poem, the *Green Eye of the Yellow God*, thought by many to be vintage Kipling, this vast and pleasantly terrifying Bhairab is the kind of image the mind associates with the frivolous whim of a colonel's daughter and the irreverent exploits of Mad Carew.

Commissioned in 1769 by King Rana Bahadur Shah, a great builder who in anguish caused more temples to be destroyed than he had built, its purpose apparently is to protect the old palace by warding off evil influences. Normally the mask can barely be glimpsed behind a carved wooden screen. But during the days of Indra Jatra and the coinciding festival of the Living Goddess, it is open to public view, its golden crown of serpents, skulls and rock-sized jewels half hidden by floral and paper decoration: the petrified smile on its golden face heightened by black, red and white paint: awesomely colossal: too magnificent to be terrifying, though its white teeth suggest sacrificial hunger and its angry eyes were designed to strike fear into evil hearts.

Young boys sit beside the scarlet mouth as if tempting providence, collecting offerings and giving *prasad* in return. Crowds form and disperse. Individuals or families perform elaborate pujas before the god. Tourists visibly stunned by so incredible a sight go wild with still and movie cameras. The best is yet to come.

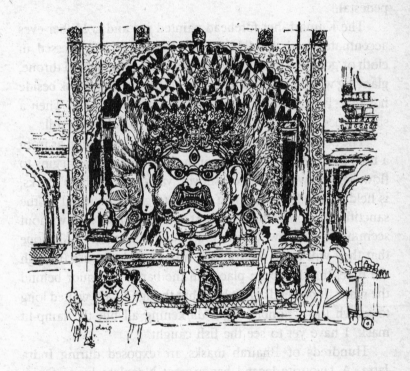

After being drawn through the streets of Kathmandu on her gilded *rath,* the Living Goddess, attended by her young escorts Bhairab and Ganesh, pauses before the great mask of the Seto Bhairab. Crowds by now are so dense it seems the Kumari's chariot will never move again. It is one of those fantastic sights that wears an aura of disbelief. The old palace on two sides, its temple towers frilled with scarlet cloth, the scarlet Hanuman under his ceremonial umbrella beside a golden gate framed by statuary, stout palace pillars carved with green, writhing snakes; soldiers in old uniforms, clouds of incense, showers of flowers and coins on the three *raths*, the great grimacing mask of Bhairab reflecting the flames of votive lamps, and temples crowding the other side, among them a golden statue of a Malla king and his four sons on a stone pedestal.

The Kumari, her forehead painted red and gold, her eyes accentuated with *kajal*, crowned elaborately and dressed in cloth of gold and scarlet silk, sits serenely on her gilded throne, glancing with ill concealed interest at the dwarfing mask beside her *rath*. Basketfuls of *prasad* are dumped about her. Then a shout goes up as the ropes go taut and the chariots roll.

The Seto Bhairab is now the sole focus of attention as from a tube protruding from his mouth, blessed rice beer begins to flow. The crowd scrambles, shoves, vaults each others' backs, is held up briefly by helping hands, to get a mouthful of the sanctified liquor. Some are expert at taking long swigs without seeming to swallow. Others are liberally drenched. All hope that they will catch the live fish tiny enough to pass through the tube, that has been placed in the barrel of liquor behind the mask. It portends great luck, but though I have waited long to watch the scramble, night darkening all but the lamp-lit mask, I have yet to see the fish caught.

Hundreds of Bhairab masks are exposed during Indra Jatra. A favourite legend has a great Nepalese king of old, Yalambar, journey to India to witness the epic battle of the Mahabharata. He went disguised as Shiva in his terrifying Bhairab form, wearing a silver mask. When Yalambar and Krishna met on the battlefield, the god of love asked the Nepalese king on which side he intended to fight. Yalambar replied that he would join the losing side, whereupon Krishna, fearing that such a move might turn the battle, swept off Yalambar's head with such force that it soared through the air and landed in the Kathmandu valley.

It is exposed to this day, a handsome silver mask, known as the Akash Bhairab. It too is honoured by a visit from the Living Goddess. The countless other Bhairab heads exposed throughout the valley have as many tales attached to them that explain the reason for the god's decapitation. I have found none that explain how the handsome Seto Bhairab lost his body.

A House for Shiva and Parvati

 It is important to remember that Kathmandu is the valley of the gods. If deities no longer descend in disguise to watch festivals, their favourite pastime, they pose as virgin children or the masked religious dancers who represent them on special occasions. I have often seen dancers so agitated by the divinity in command of them, they have had to be held by people on both sides.

In ancient Bhaktapur, the mysterious nine Durgas contrive to make themselves appear inhuman, in masks smeared with vermilion, saffron and sacrificial blood. Their gait, the exaggerated way they breathe and talk, their collective sense of secrecy set them apart. After centuries of familiarity, they are still held in awe. Kathmandu is no exception. Indra's elephant dances in streets at Indra Jatra, as do Bhairab and two attendants, also the demon Lakhe and the demoness Dogani. Should Lakhe and Dogani meet they would fight to their death, so great care is taken to keep them apart.

In the artists' city of Patan, at Dasain or Durga puja, young men impersonating the eight mother goddesses, the *ashtamatrikas*, are worshipped as real goddesses and lavishly fed. So colourful are these ceremonies that often blaze in the darkness of night, it is no wonder the gods are often tempted to drop by. It seems the great Lord Shiva himself made a habit

of coming to see the divine dances held in Kathmandu's Durbar Square. At first he came alone but it was not long before his consort Parvati pleaded to be taken along.

King Rana Bahadur Shah decided to build a pavilion befitting the pleasure of Shiva and Parvati, and so, on a raised plinth that has a grandstand view of all the many excitements that fill the old Palace Square, he had a suitable house constructed. A house it is despite its elaborate decoration. In the heavily ornamented top floor, the middle of its nine window frames are carved and painted wooden images of Shiva and Parvati in mortal form, a unique representation.

They rest on the window rail, looking out over the passing scene in a manner suggesting interest in all they see. And what wondrous things they look upon. Just across the square from them is the house of the Living Goddess. She can be seen occasionally at her gilded window or being taken in vivid procession. They have witnessed numerous coronations, two divine people in a confetti-bright crowd that fills every inch of space in the square, to watch the newly crowned king walk to pay homage at a nearby Ganesh shrine, then come by on elephant back, his queen at his side, leading a glittering procession out of wonderland.

Did they recognize other gods and goddesses masquerading as mortals in the crowd? Did they wonder at the Victorian *baithak khana* added to the old Malla architecture of the place by the Rana maharajas? Were they amazed by the first automobiles, surprised by the first foreigners and startled by the coming of the hippies?

Not far from their pavilion is a temple on a towering plinth which became a favourite abode of hippies, a smoker's paradise, a rent free rest house. The hippies went, the huge coaches with London-Constantinople-Tehran-Delhi-Kathmandu, the more frequent Kathmandu-Goa, the extraordinary Chapati Express, they all went. The trippies, the budget travellers, came.

Colourfully dressed women selling Jaipuri mirror work, old clothes, old saree borders set up shop below Shiva and Parvati. So also curio dealers, and a bicycle hire shop. Shiva and Parvati have watched them all, have posed for endless photographs and starred in many films. What they'll see next is anyone's guess. Like all capital cities, Kathmandu changes fast. But the festivals and processions will always be the same.

Women with votive offerings, men leading a sacrificial goat or playing old fashioned musical instruments will always come by at dawn and dusk. Sometimes, even in the late of night. Then unnoticed, just two people among a worshipful crowd, Shiva and his consort might leave their ornate pavilion and walk the streets of Kathmandu again.

The City Vishnu May Have Built

 Of all the ancient cities of the Kathmandu valley, Bhaktapur is the least changed. There are vistas over acres of medieval tiled roofs interrupted only by the thrust of temple spires and golden images atop tall stone pedestals. In the narrower lanes, carved wooden windows almost meet overhead. Grain is winnowed in the streets and chillies dried wherever space permits, so at times streets, temple squares and rooftops are bright scarlet. Corn and vegetables cascade from wooden eaves to dry in the wondrously golden sun of Bhaktapur. It is a farmer's city, so one surprises people laden with hay or carrying vegetables hung from bamboo yokes across their shoulders. It is not uncommon to see piled vegetables in one basket balanced by a small child or two in the other. Now small tractors have invaded the streets and lanes tremble as they pass.

There is far less Western attire about. The elderly and the old stick to their traditional dress. Women wear striking red and black sarees with white shawls, their ears outlined in gold rings. There are as yet no shops selling the enticements of Bangkok and Hong Kong. Although for a while, when the valley discovered videos, there were cinema posters stuck to ancient carved wood or left standing against guardian stone lions outside temples. Youths glued to walkmans or swinging

transistors to the rhythms of the BeeGees and Eagles, were
never a feature of Bhaktapur. The young are out in the fields,
in their unsophisticated shops, or working in Kathmandu.

In fact, when you drive into Bhaktapur, your car is a time
machine and you are back in the fifteenth and seventeenth
centuries, but endowed with the extra sensory perception of
looking into the twentieth century to which the tourists belong.
The streets are paved in herring-bone brick. You may meet the
nine Durgas, fearfully masked, who strut and dance and hold
up traffic as long as it pleases them. Their acolytes, boys
dressed in turbans and loose robes hung with heavy silver and

copper jewellery demand alms. Or your progress may be stopped by a bull fight on which bets are hurriedly placed. Shops overflow into the streets; earthen pots, vegetables, insecticides, fertilizers, brass and copper ware. On a temple plinth, a witch doctor spreads his potions such as fragments of dead animals, birds and reptiles, while making sure of business by including nails, hammers, locks and flashlights among his exotica.

Tradition has it that Lord Vishnu himself built the city in the shape of a sacred conch. Surprisingly enough, aerial photographs confirm the shell shape of Bhaktapur. More believable is the claim that Licchavi kings raised the status of a cluster of villages called Bhaktagrama, on the Tibet-India trade route, to the status of a small city over which a known king, Ananda, ruled in the late ninth century. It is recorded that at the end of the fourteenth century the well-known Malla king, Jaya Sthiti, moved his capital to Bhaktapur.

The city prospered. Mule trains jingled over the passes from Tibet. Caravans of porters came from India. One can imagine the streets filled with traders from as far as Lhasa, Shigatse, Lucknow and Benares. Spices and condiments, salt, brocades, fine cotton, silks, tea, grain, jade and porcelain, gilded images, furs, painted scrolls, arms, horses, live birds and animals for a king's menagerie. In the centre of the town was a large hostelry favoured by Tibetans, still known as the Bhote Bahal. In an outstandingly handsome temple square is a house built for Indian Brahmins imported from South India to teach and translate religious texts. The rich raised fine houses, kings lavished love and money on the city to raise temples, shrines and rest houses for pilgrims. They embellished the city with statuary and carving, extended the palace, built baths and fountains, ghats by the river and large, ornate tanks to ensure an adequate supply of water. The fame of the city spread far and wide. Because of its numerous temples and shrines and the pious nature of its people, it became known as the city of devotees.

Though once the capital of an undivided valley, Bhaktapur fell prey to the politics of ambition that not only separated the cities of Kathmandu, Patan and Bhaktapur, but had them almost continuously at war with each other. Perhaps the walls that ringed the cities belong to an earlier age when they were susceptible to attack from numerous enemies. Or they were hurriedly built when the valley divided itself into three kingdoms, each with armed satellite towns that protected the cities. Chronicles make numerous mentions of these walls, but nothing remains of them except two gates in Bhaktapur and one in Patan.

Even these are not very old. As targets of repeated attack they must have been destroyed time and time again. The western gate in Bhaktapur, surprisingly Moghul in style, is late Malla. Having seen the assault of the Gurkha king Prithvi Narayan Shah in 1767 and the unification not only of the valley but the whole of Nepal, the old gate has remained an ornament, its two stone lions guarding the city against nothing more serious than invasions of modern tourists.

Through the gate is one of my favourite views; the cobbled road dipping steeply into the medieval city so that houses are elevated on plinths and connected to the road by stone stairways. Carved wooden rest houses that must once have stood free are now part of the walls of houses, most of them housing ceremonial *raths* of various sizes. Over the rooftops looms the tiers of the temple of the five sages, Bhaktapur's proudest monument. And beyond, are the mountains.

The road is invariably filled with men carrying heavy loads of vegetables, hay and pottery. Time stands still. One looks into the high noon of Newari art and culture. Into a wondrous age that has left so many brilliant monuments behind.

Only the lampposts and the Mercedes Benz relic remind of the present.

A Golden Gateway for a Goddess

 Having built a palace of ninety-nine courtyards and a forest of exquisitely carved windows, the kings of Bhaktapur had one important ambition to fulfil: to build a gateway worthy of the royal goddess Taleju Bhawani. Ancient chronicles do not record which master craftsmen were commissioned to create so demanding an undertaking. Whoever they were, they created what eminent art historians believe to be the single most beautiful and precious monument in the valley of Kathmandu. They chose copper with which to fashion images so fabulous, so delicate, so divinely beautiful that they well may be, believe those who see this masterpiece, the work of the gods themselves. To the copper they fused gold by secret processes several centuries old so that the whole splendid structure may well have been fashioned from the precious metal.

In fact, much of the Golden Gate is made of mellow brick and I find it incongruous that so priceless a gem should be set in such base material. But then brick is the substance of Bhaktapur; beautiful russet brick that glows like old copper in the mountain sun. It paves lanes and streets and courtyards; it frames treasures of carved wood. So, why not metal, however precious? Brick is of the rich soil of Bhaktapur, a part of romantic and turbulent history. Then again, the Golden

Gate is almost a temple in itself, the brick walls supporting a golden pagoda roof and an extravagance of golden finial: a many-tiered sacred golden canopy, frills and scarves of gold. Temple banners surmounted by deities. Rampant lions. Elephants. Dragons. And tinkling ornamented hangings that might be the earrings of the goddess. All golden.

Above the entrance is a tympanum or *torana* upon which, seething about the central figure of Taleju Bhawani, are a gilded protectiveness of deities and divine beasts. Ganga and Jamuna. Garuda. Water nymphs. Serpents. Lions. A tortoise. A crocodile. The sun and the moon. All held together by heavenly plants and celestial fires. And all, all of them, gold.

On either side of the doorway are pillars embellished with images of divinities supportive of Taleju Bhawani and sacred *kalashs,* pitchers and two inscribed tablets. All made from gold.

The Golden Gate is credited to King Jaya Ranajit Malla who ordered it built in 1753. But since records suggest that the gate and the courtyard into which it leads, known as Mul Chowk, took three centuries to complete, it is almost certain that there were other gates less worthy of the goddess or, perhaps, as beautiful, that perished in the earthquakes that so often destroyed Bhaktapur. What is more important than the actual splendour of this gate is the depth of religious feeling that caused it to be made. Taleju Bhawani, a goddess who has her origin in distant south India, was joyously welcomed by the kings of Nepal when she was brought to the valley in the early fourteenth century. Not only was she enthusiastically received but accepted as the royal household goddess for whom uniquely lavish temples were built in the palaces of Bhaktapur, Patan and Kathmandu. It is recorded that the Karnatak king who brought Taleju Bhawani to the valley either ruled, or lived as a royal guest in Bhaktapur. And so it was in Bhaktapur that the goddess was first enshrined.

It is interesting that despite their individual heights the three temples to Taleju Bhawani are the same height above the valley floor, so that in Bhaktapur which is on a plateau, the temple is much squatter than the one in Patan, while in low lying Kathmandu (fourteen kilometres from Bhaktapur) the temple soars grandly on several massive plinths. This, it is believed, made it easy for the goddess to travel between her three temples. It is recorded that before the advent of modern buildings and pollution, it was possible to see the temples of Taleju from one city or another despite the distance in between.

Just outside the Golden Gate is a great bell which to this day is rung whenever prayers are offered to Taleju Bhawani. And a short walk away from the gate is a small monastery built about a courtyard where the virgin goddess, Kumari, who is an earthly emanation of Taleju Bhawani, used once to reside. She now lives in the palace beyond the Golden Gate. A plaque in the monastery claims that this was where the cult of the Living Goddess, Kumari began, a claim that would surely be disputed heatedly by Kathmandu.

About the gate there is no dispute. Though Kathmandu and Patan also have golden gates for the goddess Taleju, Bhaktapur's is the most spectacular. Also the most familiar, because where the others are inaccessibly high above the streets, the jewel of Bhaktapur, the Golden Gate, has its feet in the dust of Durbar Square.

Was There a Yeti in the Royal Zoo?

 In a corner of Bhaktapur's Durbar Square, standing prominently below the old palace, is a small shikara type temple to Bhagwati, significant because it boasts some amazing sculpture. Images of the goddess are particularly fine, but eclipsed by a double row of stone statues that flank the temple stairway.

At the base are two strong men, perhaps watchmen or royal guards. They restrain savage mastiffs with heavy chains, and in their free hand clutch what have been described variously to me as children or criminals. I favour children because the nude figures clutch what look like balls or fruit in their hands. On the other hand, the firmness with which they are held suggests evildoers of some sort, their small size perhaps reflecting the old artistic device of making lesser characters smaller than important ones. Whatever, the dress of the larger figures is extraordinary. To me they look like Venetian Doges, but obviously they wear the costume of the court. Very grand headdresses wound around with figured turbans and secured with jewelled clasps. Carefully pleated robes, handsome belts in which are tucked daggers, Tibetan type boots and a wealth of jewellery around their necks and cascading from their ears.

I asked passers-by as I sketched if they knew who these figures represented and the answers were fascinating.

Wrestlers. Policemen. Royal ayahs. Gods. Zoo keepers. Executioners. Noblemen. The child was being punished, dragged for a walk, going to be killed, fed to the dog. Since the child, or criminal, wears a sort of coronet on its head, guessing becomes difficult.

Above the men are two horses, richly caparisoned, hung with bells, bejewelled, and even their hooves appear to be carved, perhaps painted with bold designs. These surely were royal mounts, or more important, mounts fit for the gods. They look spirited without a trace of devilment.

With the two one-horned rhino above the horses, we are into conjecture again. Were these primordial beasts brought from the Terai in the heavy chains they wear to fight before the king, or were they exhibits in his zoo? That they wear rich saddle cloths seems to suggest that they may have been tame and used especially for processions. The anonymous sculptor, however, has captured a meanness in their eyes that together with their heavy chains makes me believe they belonged either to a royal menagerie or were watched in duels, distinguished by the colours they wore.

Sitting above the rhino are the most intriguing of all the sculptures. Undoubtedly they portray wild-men, jungle-men, ape-men or could they possibly be yetis? They have human faces with beards, manes and moustaches. But their ears are pointed, like animals, their bodies are as much animal as they are muscular human. The way in which they crouch rather than sit points to the wild. And they wear heavy chains of captivity. Is it possible that a Malla king had ape-men in his zoo, or had the sculptor either himself seen or heard the tales of wild men of the snows?

Lastly are a pair of camels, the only two stone sculpted camels in the Kathmandu valley. In fact, it is only in Bhaktapur, carved into an ornate wooden window and here on the steps of the Bhagwati temple, that camels have inspired sculptors and carvers. Could it be they echo the camel caravans that crossed the high Gobi desert on their way to Tibet and Nepal? Or do they recall the camels of the Rajputana desert that the early Rajput immigrants remembered?

I have been unable to discover the purpose of these delightful sculptures other than that they protect the deity in the temple. Many of the great temples of Bhaktapur have their entrances guarded by legendary wrestlers of superhuman strength. One memorable example has the ascending humans, beasts and divinities each ten times stronger than the other so that the accumulative strength protecting the temple image is enormous.

This Durga temple was raised in the seventeenth century, in all probability by the master builder of Bhaktapur, King Bhupatindra Malla. His love of the beautiful and bizarre may well make him responsible for this temple and its unique sculpture.

If only he had kept a diary. I'd love to know about that ape-man. That yeti.

The Temple of the Trinity

Legend has the temple to Dattatraya in Bhaktapur built from the wood of a single tree and seldom has a tree been put together again so reverently. For me, there still is the dark feel of forest in the temple that I find a little intimidating. But this darkness only enchances the stone figures and gilded symbols which adorn the front of the temple: two powerful humans armed with shields and bludgeons; and the *chakra* and conch stood upon stone pedestals, supported by turtles. Facing the temple, on another higher stone pedestal, is a splendid, golden Garuda, kneeling in prayer. Strangely, among these emblems of Vishnu is Shiva's trident, for Dattatraya, a popular deity in south India, represents a trinity of Vishnu, Shiva and Brahma.

There are at least two schools of thought on how this deity came to Kathmandu. He could have been brought by the Karnataka kings who made Bhaktapur their home in the early fourteenth century, and were responsible for introducing the royal goddess Taleju Bhawani to the Kathmandu valley, or Dattatraya may have been brought by an influx of south Indian Brahmins who the Malla kings invited to Nepal to teach and interpret the Hindu doctrines.

The construction of the temple is attributed to the famous King Yaksha Malla who reigned over a unified valley, in the

fifteenth century. Bhaktapur was never so important, so
wealthy and so powerful, but architecturally speaking the age
of lavish decoration had not arrived. The temple to Dattatraya,
though unique in being the only one of its kind in the valley
of Kathmandu, is sparsely ornamented. There are some
handsome angels, a motif common in Bhaktapur, on the
façade that suggest a Persian influence. The scalloped arches
bring Muslim architecture to mind, but there are also Chinese
lions and dragons — an amalgam of motifs that underscore

the fact that Bhaktapur stood upon the crossroads of strong and widely differing cultures.

The erotic sculpture seen so commonly in Nepalese temple architecture, has several interpretations, but three are worthy of projection. Lightning is a virgin goddess who would be far too ashamed to strike a building adorned with erotic art. Delightfully fanciful a story though this is, it is quite amazing that the valley's lofty temples, crowned by metal finials, are seldom if ever struck. Another theory has erotic sculpture being a deliberate temptation to test the piety of those visiting temples, and yet another has it as an attempt to encourage reproduction in an age of underpopulation and drastic infant mortality.

The two massive stone figures guarding the entrance to the temple have a colourful place in folklore. They were famous wrestlers, credited with the strength of ten normal people — ideal *dvarpalas* for a temple so important. Wrestling was a great sport of the times. The story goes that one day as the king was enjoying a bout of wrestling, word was brought to him of the birth of his son. He immediately bestowed the title Malla, meaning wrestler, on the infant, and it was used thereafter.

All about the temple, facing onto the beautiful square, are *maths* and handsome buildings that testify to the importance of Dattatraya. Here is the pujari *math*, one of the most outstanding examples of Newari wood-carving in all of Kathmandu valley. Each of its many windows is more beautiful than the other, culminating in the most famous of all, the peacock window. Time and successive earthquakes so eroded these fine buildings, they were in danger of terminal decay when help arrived in the form of West German expertise and money. The Dattatraya temple was painstakingly taken apart and put together again. The many arts and crafts of Bhaktapur, long languishing for want of patronage, were coaxed into renaissance and not found wanting. Testifying to the skills of Nepalese and Germans who worked side by side to restore the temple and several of the buildings about the square, is the timeless look of what they have achieved. The old and the new has been so perfectly matched, so brilliantly blended, it is almost impossible to say which is the work of the fifteenth and seventeenth century builders and which the art of modern restorers.

If lightning is indeed a virgin goddess ashamed of striking temples adorned with erotic sculpture, earthquake obviously is not. The chances are it will return to tumble the many splendoured monuments of Bhaktapur. When it does, it will find the restored areas of the city bolstered against its attack and should temple, *math* or palace crumble again, there are new detailed blueprints to ensure faithful reconstruction.

It was the present head of the West German project who, stopping me as we walked through the square one day of golden sunlight said with enormous feeling, 'You know, this must be one of the most beautiful medieval squares in the world.' To which might well be added the refrain, it is this, it is this, it is this.

The Courtyard of a Thousand Delights

Legend has the priests arriving on flying white horses, all the way from south India. What a sight that must have been, the riders themselves in white, garlanded perhaps with flowers, holding the implements of worship in their hands. If indeed they rode, it was along the old trade route from India, through the dense jungles of the Terai, through the often fatal miasma of the *awal* as malaria was then called, past forts and over passes until there, before them, was the emerald valley, and Bhaktapur its capital. Or they came piously on foot, religious teachers charged with an important mission — to interpret and teach the Hindu scriptures.

They were summoned by a famous Nepalese king, received with honour and housed near the temple to Dattataraya, a south Indian deity. A sanyasi, Ramadatta Giri, probably the temple's priest, had a suitable residence commissioned for them, a building of several courtyards and a façade of amazing beauty, known as the pujari *math*.

I wonder, as he watched the mellow brick walls rise and the carvers labour over their wood, if he considered his creation to be one of the Nepal's noblest houses. Its proportions are superb, its amazing exhibition of carved,

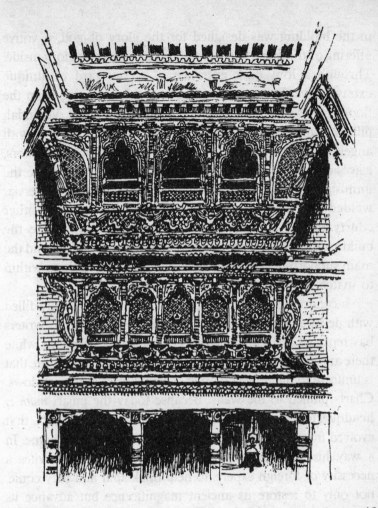

wooden windows, masterly. Though almost every motif
known to Newari art was used, and used lavishly, the main
theme is the peacock. It graces several of the many windows,
but in one it dances supreme, the Mona Lisa of Newari
woodcarving.

I find it interesting that this eighteenth century masterpiece
looks into a lane so narrow it is difficult to view it comfortably.
Perhaps the beholder was of secondary consideration if he was
considered at all. The window, like all the exquisite wood work

The Courtyard of a Thousand Delights **/ 77**

in the building was designed for the glory of god, a votive offering of the finest talent extant. There is greater glory inside. Through a low, dark entrance is a courtyard of unique extravagance. Every inch of the four sides, starting from the floor to the second storey roof projection, is carved. Verandah pillars, banked windows, lintels, cornices are all filigreed with angels, dragons, serpents, animals, birds, branches, flowers, leaves and a bewildering array of pure design. There are the unmistakable influences of India, China and the old Persia, welded together in a style distinctly Newari. The other courtyards are almost bare of ornamentation. Inside the building the ceilings are head-threateningly low. Pillars and the main supporting beams are carved, but there is nothing within to match the beauty of the exterior.

Incongruously, several of the long, low rooms are now filled with desks and office chairs. The clackety buzz of typewriters has replaced the sound of prayer. Instead of priests in white there are Germans and modern Nepalese in the casual attire that is uniform to the project worker. There is glass in the windows. Charts pinned to the walls. Because today the pujari *math* is headquarters to the Bhaktapur Development Project that evolved from the original West German restoration scheme. In a way history is being repeated. A Nepalese king invites a necessity of foreign experts to help Bhaktapur and they come, not only to restore its ancient magnificence but advance its essential requirements — things like modern sanitation, schools, paved roads, a sewage system and training in new skills while the old are encouraged. So impressive has this effort been that last year Bhaktapur won an international heritage award.

Quite something for a city that just a few years ago was knee deep in decay.

A Decapitated God and an Insatiable Princess

 No one knows exactly how old the temple is. It probably began with a small shrine to Bhairab, the god of terror, and slowly, as the city of Bhaktapur grew, it was given the status of a temple. Tradition has it originally a large, single storey construction which could account for three otherwise inexplicable finials where the ground floor meets the first. Its importance is never in doubt, whether as a small shrine, a single storey temple or the present majestic edifice that occupies one whole side of an important Bhaktapur Square. Because, if legend is to be believed, the temple originally enshrined not a metal or wooden replica, but the actual head of the god himself.

It seems Bhairab came from Benares where he is identified with the Shiva of Kashi Viswanath, to watch the famous festival of Bisket disguised as a mortal. A tantric priest of unusual perception recognized the god, and wishing to keep him in Bhaktapur began binding him with powerful spells. In desperation, the god began to sink into the earth but not before the tantric quickly cut off his head. A trophy so sacred required a suitable shrine, so it was carried, dripping blood, to the temple in Taumaudhi Square where it was installed with great rejoicing. Wherever the blood had fallen was marked with large stones that were worshipped as shrines. They are still in the streets today, reddened with vermilion, but no longer so sacred they may not be stepped upon or driven over. Medieval Bhaktapur grows suddenly modern and its religion moves with the times. Restoration, for instance must forget taboos like unbelievers not entering the holiest precincts. Purification ceremonies are conducted and the work goes on.

Records suggest that the Bhairab temple was commissioned by King Bhupatindra Malla (1690-1722), a connoisseur of art and a great builder, but there is another, more romantic story. The king, never tired of beautifying his city, felt that the existing Bhairab shrine did little credit to its unique importance. So he ordered two more floors to be added to the temple, to be topped with a gilded roof and golden finials. Instead of being pleased by all this royal extravagance, the god grew angry at being disturbed. He caused earthquakes, drought and pestilence to threaten the city. The worried king consulted his astrologers and soothsayers and they finally came up with extraordinary advice. To appease the furious deity, the king must build a temple for Bhairab's consort that must be of singular beauty and size. Only then would the god be satisfied.

It was done at last. The temple was built, the angry Bhairab appeased. At least until 1934, when a severe earthquake that devastated Bhaktapur made a ruin of the temple. It has been faithfully restored, so that few if any looking at it today would doubt it being centuries old.

During Bhaktapur's spectacular Bisket festival, the image of Bhairab is drawn through the streets in a heavy wooden *rath*. All of Bhaktapur turns out to watch or take a turn at pulling on the ropes. Or they help raise an enormous pole at the beginning of the festival and lower it at the end. The pole and the festival recall an amazing story. There was in Bhaktapur an insatiable princess who demanded a new lover every night. Normally the men of the city would have felt privileged to

oblige, but strangely no man, however strong survived the experience. Every morning there was the sad procession of mourners taking away a son or brother or husband. The city became muted with grief. At the speed at which they were dying there would soon be no menfolk left in the city.

One day, in the very best tradition of fairytales, a handsome stranger rode into town. Unknown to anyone, he was naturally a prince. The stranger, seeking shelter for the night, happened upon an old lady convulsed with grief who between her lamentations told the prince the story of the demanding princess. That very night her only son was to present himself to the palace and the next morning she would go to collect his body. The prince gallantly promised to take her son's place, and did.

The princess was beautiful. It was love at first sight, but the prince was as clever as he was handsome. After the princess fell asleep, he quickly hid himself in a corner of the room, sword in hand. To his horror, two serpents writhed from the princess's nostrils, growing larger all the while, and obviously in search of their prey. In a flash the prince was upon them, severing their evil heads from their bodies. In the morning, when the old woman leading a procession of mourners came to collect his body, there was the prince happily hand in hand with the princess. Great were the celebrations. Bisket was born, and Bhaktapur lived happily ever after.

The wheels of the great Bhairab chariot are stacked under the eves of the temple. Sometimes, when the crowds at Bisket grow boisterous, battle zooms in the square. At other times processions converge on the temple, pujas are performed, a knife flashes and a sacrifice is made. A tourist rides a guardian lion to be photographed. Something is always happening. Like models from Singapore showing the latest fashions from Rome and Paris. Or a film unit filming an epic. Life about the temple is so interesting, one begins to scrutinize handsome strangers. Could one of them possibly be...?

A Monument to an Angry God

 Bhaktapur's greatest patron of the arts, King Bhupatindra Malla, probably had it built as a culminating edifice, a pagoda type temple to outshine all others, a monument worthy of the goddess Siddhi Lakshmi and incidentally himself. So in the heart of ancient Bhaktapur in 1702, he had the towering Nyatapola built. Then it must have been a wonder of the times. Its five elegantly soaring tiers are set upon five ascending plinths, a masterpiece of proportion and artistry that gives to the massive building an impression of gem-like delicacy. The wood carving is superb, each one of the 108 struts illustrating the numerous forms of Bhagwati Mahishamardini and lesser deities. Doors, windows, recesses, are all lavishly carved and painted. Every tier is hung with wind bells. A golden finial crowns the temple.

Even the people of Bhaktapur are uncertain about the main deity of the temple. To many she is so powerful, so secret, she is nameless and without form. To most she is Siddhi Lakshmi, to others Bhairabi, the consort of Bhairab, Lord of Terror. There is known to be a beautiful sculpture of Mahishamardini in the inner sanctum but the temple is seldom open and only select priests are permitted inside.

Leading to the main door of the temple is a steep flight of stairs flanked by pairs of massive stone figures. In ascending

order they are powerful human wrestlers, armed with bludgeons and shields, elephants, lions, griffins and the deities Simhini and Byaghrini. Each is considered to be ten times as powerful as the other and as the wrestlers have the strength of ten ordinary men the culminating protective force is that of one hundred thousand men, or several armies of the time.

But all this pales before the legend. King Bhupatindra Malla, who was forever building and beautifying his city, had the important but not impressive temple to Bhairab largely extended. To the existing rectangular shrine he had two floors added, crowning the lot with a gilded roof and a row of golden finials. Rather than being grateful, the fierce god flew into a tremendous rage at being disturbed and caused calamities unending to visit the land. There was drought and pestilence, earthquake and war. In great anguish, the king consulted his priests and astrologers who came up with an answer that must have gladdened the artistic king's heart. He must build without delay a temple to Bhairab's consort so beautiful that it would have no equal in the land.

From the forests about Bhaktapur were brought especially selected trees to which the proper sacrifices had been made. Kilns to produce the slender, rose coloured bricks and the small russet tiles for the temple, mushroomed about the city. Wood carvers, workers in metal and stone, craftsmen adept in fusing gold to copper, artists, thousands of labourers, were kept constantly at work, the king striding among them, praising and coaxing, even lending a hand. It is said that to hasten the work, the king himself led processions of workmen, carrying bricks. The temple grew. It soared. Long before it was complete its stunning beauty became legendary. More wonderful, the rain fell, the restless earth grew calm, the plagues and catastrophies that had bedevilled Bhaktapur ceased. The god Bhairab in his temple nearby was obviously satisfied.

Another version of this story has Bhairab angry, not because of being disturbed but because he resented a higher, more magnificent temple being built than his own. So he appeared to the king one night in a dream, demanding to know for whom the temple was being raised. If it was for any deity of lesser importance than himself then he would destroy not only the temple but the town. So the king's advisers had him dedicate the impressive new temple to the all-powerful Siddhi Lakshmi, and Bhairab was content.

Ironically, a temple so impressive, so legendary, is never the cause for celebration. No great processions climb its guarded stairs, no worshipful crowds throng its plinths. It stands aloof, deservedly proud, very much the lovely woman of legend ordained by a god and perfected by a king. But there is hardly a festival in Bhaktapur that does not fill the square above which the temple soars. Religious processions, dancers, musicians, *raths,* funerals, marriages, they all pass by. Sometimes the square is an arena for impromptu bull fights. Crowds collect suddenly from nowhere. Children ride the temple's guardian beasts for a better view. At the festival of cows, a Bhairab made of straw dances before his temple. And now the tourists come, taking endless photographs and browsing in the small curio shops that stand about the square.

German restorers have built a cafe in the square from the remains of an ancient pilgrim's rest house. It is a work of art in itself, its carvings faithfully reproduced, its furniture adapted from old Newari styles. From its verandahs one can watch the city go by or romanticize that one sails a galley into centuries past. Even the young proprietor is understanding. When one sits and dreams in the shadow of the Nyatapola temple, a coffee or Coke can be the slowest drink on earth.

Three Golden Kings

Among the many Nepalese kings of old, three are remembered not so much because of how they reigned or what they achieved, so much as by the very personal monuments they left behind — three golden likenesses of themselves. They kneel in the Durbar Squares of Kathmandu, Patan and Bhaktapur, atop high stone pedestals with lotus capitals for their thrones. All are attired in the finery of court dress obviously inspired by Moghul fashion: turbaned, plumed, bejewelled, belted and armed with swords, daggers and shields. All are in attitudes of devotion. Two are shaded by the hoods of rearing serpents; one by a royal parasol.

If the same master created all three, as it would seem, then he lived and worked as long as Michelangelo. Certainly he could have seen all the three kings, and beginning work on the first statue as a very young man have completed his ultimate masterpiece in his late sixties or early seventies. It was not unusual for a master craftsmen to be employed in all the three cities. And so when Pratap Malla of Kathmandu, who reigned from 1641 to 1674 decided to be immortalized in gilded metal, it is possible the sculptor went on to portray King Yoganandra Malla of Patan who occupied the throne of Patan from 1865 to 1705. Finally, he would have been summoned by the flamboyant King Bhupatindra Malla of Bhaktapur who ruled from 1697 to 1729. By then, he was a master of mature excellence who created in his likeness of the king his greatest masterpiece.

This, of course, is conjecture. Even though there were artistic exchanges between the three cities so often at loggerheads if not embroiled in open warfare, it is unlikely that a single sculptor would in fact have created the three statues, since patrons jealously guarded their master craftsmen and kings were no exception. There are the inevitable tales that have kings so delighted by the work they commissioned they had the artist either killed or maimed to avoid their masterpiece being surpassed. As inevitable are the stories that have artists knowing they would lose their eyes or hands stalling for time, usually by saying their work wasn't complete until they had made sure of their escape.

So I blatantly romanticize. A young Newari Benvenuto Cellini comes to the notice of the king of Kathmandu, known as a great poet and lover of art. He commissions a metal likeness of himself and his sons, and as it is done the king whispers orders for the artist's despatch, and the young man escapes across the river to Patan. There he does a similar life-size portrait of the king by royal command and when the time comes for his life or limbs to be endangered, he flees to the distant city of Bhaktapur. There, as an old man with all the skills of his years, he sculpts a serene likeness of the king. And there, perhaps his glorious creativity ended. But tradition has it he played on and on for time, assuring a fastidious king that his work was not quite complete until he was too old to beat and gild metal any longer. Alas, that his name does not survive with his masterpieces.

Even to this day, several lanes of Patan echo to the tap-tap-tap of metal workers creating anything from pots and pans to images of gods and goddesses. So it must have been in the past, and many could have been the masters who took their

wares and their skills to the other capital cities of Kathmandu and Bhaktapur, just as the famous woodcarvers of Bhaktapur laboured in Patan and Kathmandu.

Of the three golden kings, there is no doubt that Bhaktapur's Bhupatindra Malla is the most classically lovely. If I were permitted to choose a single masterpiece from all of Kathmandu valley's amazing treasure, without hesitation I would ask for the statue of the Bhaktapur king. He sits so lifelike, his hands gently touching in the attitude of namaskar, his shirt sleeves minutely creased, his forehead marked with vermilion, and turquoise rings still upon his fingers that it should surprise no modern beholder if he rose slowly and mounted a waiting elephant. The golden likeness matches the man, for his life was as rich as the metal he was immortalized in.

It is said that when he was a young boy he was sent by his scheming stepmother to the forests about Bhaktapur with paid assassins. So earnestly did the handsome prince plead for his life that the assassins left him with a family of Tibetan craftsmen and, dispatching a goat to bloody their knives, returned to the palace. The young prince grew strong and well versed in the arts of his foster people. And he gained sufficient popularity to lead an army on the palace, kill his usurping stepmother and her lover, and ascend the throne in triumph.

Three Golden Kings / **89**

Once crowned king, he lost no time in lavishing his love of the arts upon his city. Several of Bhaktapur's most memorable monuments arose at his command. It is said he often took an active part in their building.

Strangely, none of the succeeding Malla kings were moved to perpetuate themselves in lifelike gold. Perhaps there was already a heavy strain on their gilded purses. Or had the ultimate master cast the ultimate golden king?

Down History's Narrow Lanes

 Chillies dried and shiny red have had their time in the sun, laid out in the squares of Bhaktapur, along the sidewalks, on roofs, and cascading from wooden eaves like giant garlands. Then it was maize, spread gold and russet, or rice and ochre wheat being teased by women to ensure an even drying. Now it is green lettuce-like leaves strung in festoons to dry and preserve for future consumption. Always there are clusters of maize and garlic, and plump-yellow-pumpkins. More often than not there are pots of geranium or narcissi and the sudden blaze of azalea. When the attics overflow, planks and bamboos are laid under the eaves to accommodate boxes and baskets, farming implements and pigeon coops. The lanes of Bhaktapur are seldom without such adornment and certainly it is part of their charm, reminding one that this is one of the world's largest cities of farmers.

At daybreak a major part of the population takes to the fields, particularly during the seasons of sowing and harvesting, and returns at dusk — like processions of ghosts sometimes wading through a ground mist that lies stagnant below the city. Of Bhaktapur and its satellite town Thimi, also a community of farmers, it is said that children never recognize their fathers who are gone either to the fields or to Kathmandu with their produce long before their children are awake and return after they are asleep. That charming if pathetic story has been eroded by the coming of the Chinese highway to Tibet that sweeps past Bhaktapur, and the excellent trolley bus service between the city and Kathmandu which makes commuting not only possible but easy.

Lanes, one might blasely shrug, are lanes, are lanes the world over. What's so special about Bhaktapur? A look into history. More than a usual dollop of enchantment. A feeling as if at any moment something unexpectedly beautiful or fascinating is about to happen. Plus the very unusual art and architecture that flanks such ordinary looking city arteries. Deep wooden eaves almost meet overhead. Carved wooden balconies slant from buildings like the prows of olden ships. Windows frame masterpieces of carved wood. In the lane of my sketch is the famous peacock window and many almost as brilliant. Doorways to *maths* or important private houses are richly decorated, often flanked by carved stone lions and boasting metal doors, perhaps metal windows richly embellished with figures of deities and angels, mythical beasts or a wide-eyed squat of monkeys.

In one of my favourite lanes are pillars with elephant capitals and a door lintel carved with an amazing array of deities, among them a superb Surya on his chariot, no larger than a quarter plate. In places are carvings inlaid with ivory. In another frequented lane is the ancient Bhote Bahal, or the inn for Tibetans, where the great Tibetan king Tsrong Song Gompo might have come to sign a treaty with Nepal. Certainly traders filled the building and were entertained to Newari dancing in the paved courtyard. The famous masked dances of Bhaktapur are still performed in this building. A prancing human-legged snow lion reminds of the Tibetan connection.

Carved courtyards are a great feature of Newari architecture. They ensure privacy, protection and provide a focus for family and community feasts and pujas. Many

courtyards support small temples or shrines in front of which
stone or metal likenesses of some long-ago house owner and
his family kneel in prayer. There is a building down one of
Bhaktapur's lanes, known as Kuttu Math, which has been
painstakingly restored by the head of the West German
government-aided Bhaktapur Development Project. Its

beautiful woodwork has been cleaned and protected against further decay. Its mud-floored rooms are once again piled with local rush mats and bolsters; one of its porticos has been converted to an outdoor dining area with a table seemingly shaped from clay and baked on the spot. From a discreet picture window opened in the tiled roof is the most exciting view over medieval Bhaktapur and the mountains beyond. The twin-summited Gauri Shankar towers above them all. Most dramatic is the ancient prayer room, every inch of its walls and ceiling warm and extravagant like old brocade with a mural painting. A date has yet to be put on them, but there is nothing like them in all the city.

Gotz Hagmuller who has the vision, patience and expertise to undertake this very personal restoration says, 'The *math's* conversion for more contemporary use — while maintaining its inherited communal and religious factions — was undertaken privately in the hope that it may encourage sponsors from the private and public sector of Nepal, and from abroad, to preserve what is left of the city's rich architectural heritage.' Children attend classes in the courtyard of the *math*, their singsong lessons providing a very human background once one is used to it. On occasion, the courtyard forms a balconied theatre for local music or dance, its many levels and beautiful windows outlined in oil lamps.

As the afterglow of sunset lingers on the snow summits, the processions of shadows come home. Walking conversations. Laughter. Temple bells. A flute playing Nepalese love songs with its echo somewhere. A guitar plunking out tentative Paul Simon. That's magic enough for a lane anywhere. Even in magical Bhaktapur.

A Temple to Bhimsen, the Pandava

 For a city straddling the lucrative Tibet-India trade route, there had to be a temple dedicated to the god of trade, Bhimsen. It occupies one side of a beautiful medieval square where the caravans first stopped, where the weary rested after months of strenuous travel. So the temple's ground floor is open to all, a convenient shelter under the shrine upstairs. Where traders or pilgrims could rest. Faith or superstition had them offer prayers to the earthen deity in the temple. For their convenience, stairs descend from the building to a large tank with several freshwater springs where, to this day, people bathe and wash their clothes. Appropriately, several of the shops near the temple offer food from dark, smoke-filled interiors.

Recently, a modern type restaurant opened close by the temple offering a mixture of Nepalese, Chinese and European cuisine in the shape of fried eggs and toast. It played incessant music of similarly diverse origin; but obviously the time was not right. If Bhimsen was among the most popular gods of the seventeenth century (his temple was built in 1605) and is still venerated by businessmen, he either has lost some of his charisma or remains faithful to traders and craftsmen rather than city slickers and foreign budget-travellers. On the other hand, if legend is true, he loved food and was given to bouts of overeating. The story goes that his idol and his cult were brought in ancient times to the valley by a princess from Dolkha, a prosperous Newari village some fifty kilometres to the northeast of Kathmandu. The princess was married to a Kathmandu prince. The fierce idol of Bhimsen was among her many belongings.

Among her many followers was a massively built farmer who sported a fierce moustache. His looks, however, were deceptive, because he proved both idle and gluttonous, lying all day in the sun and consuming vast quantities of food. When his new master, the prince, upbraided him for his sluggish behaviour, the man replied that he would perform any task, however difficult, if he was given an ample basket of food to eat. Next day, to everyone's amazement, an entire large field had been filled, flooded and planted with rice seedlings, which normally was the work of hundreds, but in this case had been accomplished by the burly farmer alone. The prince, realizing that this was no mortal achievement, recognized the man for who he was, the mighty Bhimsen, and fell at his feet in worship. The farmer immediately turned to stone, to become an ever present image of the great and powerful god.

Well loved in valorous Nepal is the story of Bhimsen, one of the Pandava brothers, who was given to endless pranks involving his supernatural strength. It was he who eventually slew his evil cousin Dushasana who had degraded and defiled the Pandava's lovely wife, Draupadi. Bhimsen swore he would not rest until he had drunk the blood of Dushasana, and Draupadi similarly vowed that she would henceforth wear her hair undone until she could wash it in Dushasana's blood. Their vows were fulfilled when Bhimsen slew Dushasana and it was Krishna, who observing their bloody ritual, recognized them as having taken the forms of Bhairab, god of terror, and Bhairabi, his wrathful consort. Bhimsen,

eventually moved by his orgiastic act, undertook a severe fast on Ekadasi day, which falls in late January or early February. The day, known as Bhimsen's Ekadasi, is especially celebrated by Nepalese of the merchant classes who observe as strict fasting as Bhimsen did. Feasting naturally follows. Generous offerings are made to both Arjun, Bhimsen's gentle brother, and Bhimsen himself. Fruit, sweetmeats, lengths of cloth, eggs, flowers and coins are presented to Arjun in strict accordance with Vedic worship. The scarlet faced, fiercely moustached Bhimsen is drenched with the blood of massive sacrifice in strict keeping with tantric rites.

Bhimsen's festivals offer occasion for much feasting and merrymaking throughout Nepal. In Patan, Bhimsen's image is taken in procession through the streets of the city, preceded by bands and followed by devotees. Woe to any merchant who fails to honour his passing. In Bhaktapur, Bhimsen and his wife

Draupadi are placed in separate, canopied palanquins and carried joyously through lane and street. The sweet shops near the Bhimsen temple do brisk business. City merchants outdo each other in honouring the Lord of Trade. Tradesmen in Kathmandu believe that Bhimsen makes a journey to Lhasa every twelve years to visit and bless the Newari traders in that distant Tibetan city. A farmer is chosen to make the journey and everywhere he goes he is welcomed with feasting and presents. But most of the city's worship centres around the temple that is alleged to contain the likeness of the long ago strongman who was turned to stone as soon as he was recognized as Bhimsen.

To me, the long, low temple of Bhimsen in Bhaktapur, elaborately screened and titled, with a magnificent gilt roofed superstructure topped with golden finials, ceremonial umbrellas and gilded temple banners, is reminiscent of a river steamer becalmed beside its tank. The image is heightened by a large platform before the temple on which religious dances were performed. On a tall stone pedestal, a gilded lion stands snarling towards the temple, one paw raised in anger or salutation — the centuries have forgotten. It is appropriate that this king of the beasts, legendarily stronger than any other, should be turned to metal in front of a powerful deity who, once human, was changed to stone.

A Temple of Dubious Reputation

 The temple was first built by the great Nepalese prime minister and army commander Bhim Sen, Ochterloney's valorous opponent during the Gurkha wars of 1814-16. He planned it to be a building of singular magnificence, but the foundations were hardly complete when Bhimsen was forced to commit suicide. In accordance with popular belief of the time, it was considered inauspicious to complete an undertaking begun by someone who had died, so the temple never should have been completed. That it was owed much to the audacity of Jung Bahadur, the first Rana prime minister, Bhimsen's grandnephew who, disregarding superstition, had the temple completed. It is rumoured that he did this to atone for his part in the murder of his uncle, Mathabar Singh, and the infamous Kot massacre when hundreds of Nepal's elite were cut down at a royal audience in a single day. Apparently the victims' bodies were cremated en masse at the spot where the temple now stands. True or not, the temple even to this day is largely shunned except by temple priests, destitutes who gather to receive charity under a bequest of Jung Bahadur, or more likely his senior wife, and those who come to perform the last rites of their deceased relatives.

The imposingly large temple is set in an extensive courtyard beside the river Baghmati. It has been condemned

by many as ugly — an early Western visitor described it as too vulgar to even describe. True it has an air of being unkempt and deserted, but frankly I find it both powerful and imposing. Its style owes much to Moghul architecture of which Bhimsen was greatly enamoured. His palace, now being demolished, was Moghal in style with a fair amount of Kathmandu Gothic thrown in. His folly on the Tundikhel, Kathmandu's *maidan*, is a Muslim type minaret and his small temple near it could well have been the model for this larger, far more grand construction. Either Jung Bahadur was faithful to Bhimsen's design or had an eye for Moghul architecture himself.

The most striking aspect of the temple are four large golden griffins, a rampant, that seem to hurl themselves about into flight from the corners of the first tier of the building. They are believed to have guarded a Vishnu temple that once stood on the Tundikhel and was cleared away to make room for the large *maidan*. Crowning the high dome and giving it a Nepalese character are four gilded and plumed serpents under a sacred canopy.

In the courtyard, facing the front door of the temple, is an inscribed granite column resting on a massive stone turtle. It supports a heavily gilded, life-size statue of a man in court dress, plumed and bejewelled and wearing a sword, standing stiffly upright. He is protected from the sun and rain by a gilded canopy. History is confused as to who he is, as the highly stylized likeness makes recognition difficult. Dr Oldfield, who lived and worked in Kathmandu besides being a contemporary and friend of Jung Bahadur, describes how on 15 March 1853, a statue of the prime minister was inaugurated on the Tundikhel with a review of the army, much festivity and a grand show of fireworks. Oldfield had unpleasant things to say about the statue and thought the stone column that supported it 'peculiarly ugly.'

So we know there was a golden statue of Jung Bahadur extant and that like the temple of the golden griffins it might have been found to clutter up the new maidan and was moved elsewhere. Where better than to the temple Jung Bahadur built? Later historians, however, describe the handsome figure variously as King Rajendra Bir Bikram Shah, whose power Jung Bahadur usurped, or even his son, King Surendra Bir Bikram Shah. That the inscriptions on the stone column extol the many virtues and accomplishments of Jung Bahadur, support the belief that the statue is of the first Rana prime minister. It is a strange confusion of artistic style that links Jung Bahadur and Kings Rajendra and Surendra in death. In life there was little love lost between them.

Rajendra was deposed by Jung Bahadur and sent into exile in India. Surendra, when heir apparent, spent much astonishing ingenuity devising means of ridding himself of Jung Bahadur, who was then but an outstanding courtier. If legend is to be believed, the prince had Jung Bahadur thrown into a well from which, with the preplanned help of friends, he escaped. On another occasion, Jung Bahadur was ordered to ride his horse across a high bridge of only two poles, then turn about in the middle and ride back. His known horsemanship made the miracle possible. Then there is the great leap from the top of Bhimsen's folly which Jung Bahadur survived though his horse perished.

It was in this temple, called Kal Mochan, dedicated to the deity Satyanarayan, that in 1954 I saw the late King Tribhuvan's sons, with the exception of the eldest, King Mahendra, observe the traditional days of mourning, their heads shaved, dressed in white seamless garments, barefooted and sleeping on pallets of straw. I remember being affected then by its sense of foreboding and gloom. I still am. Little wonder then that many Nepalese mistake the gentle god of Kal Mochan for Shiva the destroyer.

On the Banks of Eternity Itself

 The lovely city of Patan is so old its origins are largely forgotten. Legend has the Buddha visit it with his beloved disciple Ananda. The great Mauryan emperor Ashoka built four stupas about the city to testify to its blessedness. From Patan, almost certainly, went the Princess Brikuti to marry the famous Tibetan king Tsrong-Song-Gompo. It is said that she took with her as her sole dowry the begging bowl of the Buddha and through her own indomitable faith caused Buddhism to take firm roots in Tibet. She comes down to us through history as the charming Green Tara, subject of countless statues and paintings.

To the Nepalese, Patan was Lalitpatan or Lalitpur, city of beauty. To Tibetan traders it was Ye Rang, which means eternity itself. The beauty remains, despite the passing of corroding centuries, destructive earthquakes, wars and the attention of vandals who sacrilegiously have wrenched some of its finest detail from the magnificence that still remains. Down every lane, in every courtyard and in the great squares are jewel-like memories of the past which, I like to think, serve as inspiration to the large number of artists and workers in wood and metal who inhabit the city. They were known to be there, feeding a flourishing Indo-Tibet trade route, when whatever there was of the ancient city was rebuilt by King

Veera Deva in the year AD 299. It is not known whether he built the wall about the city that remains only in the briefest snatches or whether it was there already, a bastion not only against invasions but nocturnal intruders. The city also had the protection of a river, more holy than protective since there are seasons when it is almost dry.

It is across this sacred river, at the confluence of the Baghmati and the Manuhara, that traders and visitors from the north came, over a medieval bridge of stout wooden beams, brick and earth. It still is easy to imagine their awe and amazement at first sight of the city with its piled pagoda roofs, golden finials flashing in the sun, its stupas and temples across the river. If they had a teller of tales travelling with them, or met a priest from any of numerous temples crowding the ghats, they would have been told that gods and goddesses came to bathe unseen at the confluence known as Shankhamul. One knew they were there when the water suddenly stopped in its glide southwards and sometimes even reversed direction. A couple of years ago an adventurous truck tried to cross the ancient bridge. I was assured by a garrulous priest that it must have chosen just the moment of the celestial dip to profane the happening. The old bridge fell apart in anguish and no one has bothered to put it together again.

Dominating this particular approach to Patan — there is another downstream where a new bridge and highway obliterate the old crossing between Kathmandu and Patan — is the temple of Jagat Narayan, nineteenth century new, and not very attractive except for four powerful images that face its entrance. Three of them, massively carved in stone as if they intend to sit out the centuries, are under metal canopies. They represent Ganesh, Garuda in his human form, and Hanuman. I have yet to find someone who will date these images that to me appear much older than the temple whose courtyard they occupy. Perhaps they were already there, open to the elements,

adding their blessings to the sacred confluence. Perhaps they graced a far older temple long since destroyed and swept away. For, to me, they have the same quality as the colossal statues of Garuda and Bhairab in Kathmandu. Behind the kneeling Garuda, atop a tall stone pillar supported on the back of a stone turtle, is a gilded Garuda, bird-faced and horned and wearing a plume of flames. He crouches, which is unusual, giving the impression of immediate flight on golden wings. A small boy who watched me sketch and claimed that his name was Amitabh Dharmendra, seemed to have the same idea. As I drew the perched Garuda he clapped his hands and shooed loudly as he would a wayward chicken. 'If he flies away,' he said 'you cannot sketch him.' If he flies away, I said in reply, we will both die of shock. The boy ran off to share his joke with a group of other children, no doubt called Zeenat, Hema and Mithun.

The temple was built by Colonel Jagat Shumshere Jung Kunwar Rana, brother of the famous Prime Minister Maharaja Jung Bahadur, in 1860. Ten years ago he had accompanied his brother to England and Europe and by doing so had disregarded the taboo of crossing the *kala pani*. Some believe he built this temple to Narayan to atone for his sin, while others see it as an attempt to keep up with his famous brother who was planning to build a temple at Kal Mochan in Kathmandu. Perhaps he was merely gifting to Patan a new temple as the culmination of a great deal of building and rebuilding he had done in the area. Several smaller temples and an imposing stretch of burning and bathing ghats owe their origin to the pious colonel, whether easing a guilty conscience or attempting to immortalize himself. Certainly the four handsome images will perpetuate his name.

A Courtyard to the Buddha's Memory

Permitting legend, it says, Gautam Buddha visited the valley of the gods to worship and teach soon after he attained enlightenment. That some of his disciples visited Kathmandu is recorded in Buddhist scriptures which mention an exchange of messages between the Buddha and Ananda. The barefooted disciples were so tortured by the rocky paths and the intense cold of the Kathmandu valley, they asked permission to wear shoes. This was granted by the Master after much apparent consideration. No record of his visit to the valley exists other than what hearsay attaches to incidents and hallowed spots. Like a small courtyard in Patan.

History would support Patan's claim to being a well-founded city at the time of the Buddha. Legend has him received by the king of Patan with much rejoicing, festivity and display of largesse. The saintly Buddha declined the gifts heaped upon him by the king and his nobles, but he accepted a simple gift of food from an old woman and blessed her for it. Humbled by this incident, the king forsook his royal living and labouring for many days as a blacksmith and gave his earnings to the poor. When the Buddha heard of this royal penance, he baptized and blessed the king who came to him as a poor craftsman and at the same time blessed and honoured the entire caste of blacksmiths. Disputed, but widely upheld, is the belief that he bestowed upon them his own name, Sakya.

There is in Patan today a small courtyard built about a Buddhist *chaitya* which is believed to be the spot where this memorable event took place. Kneeling at the foot of the *chaitya* and facing the door of a small chapel are the stone figures of a man and two women simply attired, their hands folded in homage. Could they be the king and his consorts? The courtyard is known as Dhum Baha and once a year the blacksmiths of Patan congregate here to celebrate, just as once a year a festival of feasting and worship centres about the place where the old woman blessed by the Buddha lived. I asked some people living in the courtyard about the history of the place. The two women sunning themselves said it was very important and wonderful but they couldn't remember what it was. A child thought the kneeling stone figures were his grandfather and aunts. I might have imagined the amused look on the face of the all-seeing Buddha on a stupa overlooking the courtyard.

So wondrous a story is surely built on fact, though there were scholars who cast doubt upon the Buddha ever having visited the Kathmandu valley. They would have us believe that the visit of the Mauryan emperor Ashoka centuries later is also unfounded, despite the fact that he is credited with building four stupas about the city of Patan to testify to its blessedness. They are still extant, three of them simple grass-covered mounds as they must have been when they were first built, and one encased in plaster with a painted spire. Interestingly, this embellished stupa stands close by the old bridge over which Tibetan traders came to Patan. One can imagine the offerings they lavished on so holy a shrine. Then there is the unshakable story that Ashoka gave his daughter Charumati in marriage to

a local prince. Between them they raised the city of Deopatan, a conch call away from the great temple of Pashupatinath. Charumati was also responsible for building a vihara and stupa at adjoining Chabahil. The existing vihara though ancient has certainly not seen two centuries, but the stupa, if it were to yield up its secrets, would surely remember the pious princess.

A Courtyard to the Buddha's Memory / **109**

The heaviest concentration of Buddhists and Buddhist monuments is in Patan. The Sakyas are a prominent Buddhist caste. It is from among the Sakyas that the Virgin Goddess Kumari is selected. The Sakyas still shape wondrous images and work in metal. The sound of beaten metal fills many a Patan lane. But sadly the Sakya craftsmen are dying out. 'There is not much future in the business,' a young Sakya graduate told me. 'The demand for fine arts and crafts is rapidly decreasing. Even the handmade household utensils my people produced are being replaced by factory-made products. Our young are turning to the import-export business. Or doing jobs like I'm doing. I'm an agriculturist, with honours from foreign universities. When I have nothing better to do I take tourists around. I speak two foreign languages.'

The young man took me to a nearby temple being shuttered against the night. 'Not long ago this place was open night and day. Now, even though we lock the gates there is the fear of thieves coming over the rooftops.' Did he believe in the Buddha's coming?

'That's an awfully long time ago,' he said.

Patan's Monastery Fantastic

 Confusing as my sketch is the monastery itself. All about the entrance to the inner shrine is the most amazing collection of statuary: Trafalgar lions, Nepalese lions, *garudas, shadruls,* squatting elephants and dancing peacocks. There is also an impressive gathering of deities and adding to the strange concourse is a life-size statue of a Rana prime minister in full regalia. The likeliness is hardly flattering, the style primitive, the proportions so obviously out that the story of the maharaja prime minister taking one look and saying a firm no to the statue being installed in the palace secretariat is easily believable. Apparently, the sorely crushed sculptor made a votive offering of his work to the monastery, and there it remains. The other story has the prime minister donating a likeliness of himself in recognition of some divine indulgence, regardless of the company he would keep.

It is safe to say that no device old, middle-aged or modern has failed to find a place in Patan's Uku Bahal, also known as Rudra Varna Mahavidhara. Two huge rampant lions above the outer entrance gate remind strongly of the British coat-of-arms. The door knockers are lion heads holding heavy bronze rings in their mouths. There are other lions, small and big, doing things like holding pendents or acting as mounts to shapely goddesses. A Malla king kneels in prayer before the main shrine with a *garuda* on a pedestal immediately behind him. On the first tier of the two-roofed building is a group of plaster stupas. On the second is a line of handsome, gilded *chaityas*. The struts supporting the first roof depict the five Mahabuddhas and date to 1653 when they were donated to the shrine. No one knows exactly when all the other offerings were made. As an elderly gentleman who watched me sketch said pointing to an ancient lady, sunning herself in a doorway, 'She has seen much, but even she is unknowing of all this.' 'Oh no,' she countered, wheezing alarmingly. 'I remember the prime minister being put here. It took a lot of deciding where he should be placed. He gave much money to the monastery.'

Though looking fairly modern, particularly because of its European lions, Uku Bahal is alleged to have been built by the Licchavi king Siva Deva in the sixth century for the performance of his initiation rites, a custom followed by several later Licchavi kings of Patan. For reasons that have failed to survive the centuries, the practice was discontinued until King Rudra Malla revived it in the thirteenth century. Some of the exquisite wood carving, like several struts depicting willowy goddesses standing upon dwarfs or demons, date to the early fourteenth century. So does a *torana* over the main door of the temple which enshrines an image of Gautama Buddha. Apparently Patan's master woodcarvers, metalworkers and sculptors in stone contributed their skill to this incredible monastery, a gesture apparently discontinued for lack of patronage or perhaps out of consideration for space. There is hardly room for another peacock or legendary beast.

All about Uku Bahal are the homes and workshops of metalworkers, tap-tapping out household utensils, and the vessels of worship. There also are image makers using the ancient lost wax process. Many are now mass-producing gods and goddesses for foreign markets, which unfortunately shows in the finish of their creations. But there still are the master

craftsmen, too few for lack of discerning demand, who labour over the most intricate designs. Any of them could reproduce the fantastic figures of Uku Bahal, or the huge metal arch of entwined leaves and flowers that rises in front of the temple, above goddesses riding lions that in turn ride elephants. In the many atelier shops about the monastery are enticing caves of treasure still being produced by the artisans of the city of artists. If one had the inclination and money today, there is no doubt at all in my mind that the craftsmen about Uku Bahal would raise an equally stunning if not more grandiose masterpiece. Instead, they lament the passing of foreign demand and the near collapse of local patronage.

In an effort to utilize the skill of Patan's metalworkers, a couple of well-known entrepreneurs took on the manufacture of objects quite foreign to Nepalese design. An Egyptian cat. A Greek horse. For a while the rejects found their way into local curio shops. Then they disappeared because, no doubt, the demand dried up. It is a pity that examples of this period in Patan's creativity weren't enshrined in Uku Bahal. As the elderly gentleman who watched me sketch to the end observed, 'People are not as rich or generous or pious as they were.' Amen.

In the Heart of Eternity Itself

At the centre of Patan is its Durbar Square, a massive, living museum of architecture and art that is endlessly wondrous. For here, treasure is heaped on treasure. Palaces and temples stand harmoniously together as if the builders of many centuries were following a plan conceived when the city was young — a time unhesitatingly described as when gods walked the earth. Historians have the city rebuilt by King Veera Deva in the year AD 299. It was a flourishing city when the Emperor Ashoka visited it in about 250 BC, and an impressively large one as measured by the stupas that Ashoka had raised at its cardinal points. The city was apparently built in the shape of a *chakra,* one of the sacred emblems of Vishnu. The planning of its streets and its water and sewage system were ahead of the times. For sheer beauty it was unrivalled. To this day, one has only to stand at the entrance to the Durbar Square to gaze upon Eternity Itself — a description of the city so aptly given by Tibetan traders of olden times.

Along one side of a far reaching square is the Royal Palace, apparently begun in the fourteenth century but almost certainly resting on older foundations. What an incredible pile it is — of brick and carved wood pierced with golden doors and exquisite windows. Pagoda roofs, many of them gilded and with golden finials, tower one above the other to culminate in the seven storied temple of Teleju, the royal goddess. Opposite the palace, almost filling the square, are temples in stone, brick and wood that are each a masterpiece of its particular age and style. Two stone *shikara* type temples, both dedicated to Krishna, commemorate two widely differing events. One, the sati of eight queens, the wives of King Yoganarendra Malla whose golden statue sits atop a stone pillar in the square, and the other a king's romantic dream. The latter temple tells, in exquisite stone carving, the entire stories of the Mahabharata and Ramayana. It is built on the spot where King Siddhi Nara Singh Malla dreamed he saw Krishna and his consort Radha making love. Before it, on a high lotus pedestal, sits the most beautiful of *garudas* with luminous crystal eyes.

The present contributes pulsating life to what could be an intimidating square. A modern breed of curio dealers spread their wares under huge guardian stone lions and elephants on tiered temple plinths or on platforms designed for public *durbars* and public entertainment. I have often watched heroic dramas being performed in front of the Teleju temple by petromax lamps and erratic electric lights. By day, huge tourist coaches force the square and camera-laden foreigners are almost as numerous as locals. About the sati temple hill people invariably congregate in a riot of uninhibited colour. The women wear bright beads and coin necklaces. Saucer sized gold earrings. Flower shaped nose rings. Gaudy head shawls. Vivid waist bands. Men sport jaunty caps and rough woollen jackets, their song and laughter prompted both by a warming drink and the intoxicating atmosphere of Patan.

The other, more splendid Krishna temple of the royal dream, is as surely thronged with devotees from south India, mostly solemn, often garrulous. Children, well-versed in the ways of modern tourists and speaking a smattering of several languages, pose happily for photographs after the inevitable

introduction of 'Hello, one rupee.' This salutation is not to be confused with begging. It is a mere thrust into the great unknown world of the outside and is invariably followed by a conversation something like this:

You where from?

Germany.

West or East?

West.

Capital Bonn, okay?

Okay.

You American?

Yes.

Capital Washington D.C.

Right on.

Okay, bye bye, one rupee.

I stood in the shadow of two temples to do my sketch, one dedicated to Narayan and the other, the royal love temple, dedicated to Krishna. In no time I was surrounded by the curious but my view was well guarded by a large Nandi that was from time to time used as a grandstand by children. Ahead of me, in golden silhouette against the tall rise of the Teleju temple, was the lovely Garuda, kneeling reverently in prayer, hands and wings folded, serpents poised about his face. Beyond him, also on a lotus pedestal, was King Yoganarendra Malla, shaded by a rearing serpent. On the head of the serpent sits a bird and thereby hangs a tale worth telling. The king, tired of his royal living, decided to go into retreat in some distant place from which he never returned. But legend has it that before he left his sorrowing court and people, he promised he would return so long as the gilded bird perched upon the gilded serpent. A window of this palace is still kept open against his return and until a few years ago his bed and hookah stood ready for his instant use.

A bamboo scaffolding begins to spread across the face of the old palace, giving a welcome assurance that this treasury of Newari art is being restored. If the bird knew where to go, it might fly wildly away to tell the old Malla king the good news. And return again to add its romantic tale to a wondrously romantic square.

No Water in the Royal Bath

 I admit to being terrified by Sundari Chowk in the old Malla palace of Patan. Not physically, but as an artist. The wealth of design, the amazing detail, the intricate perspectives have foiled many an attempt to sketch or paint the royal bath that lies at the centre of the courtyard. Besides, the continuous stream of tourists is intimidating. There is just so much one can take of having one's work critically scrutinized in several languages. So when I had to I went late, at a time when the great tourist coaches are pointed back towards Kathmandu. And I went with determined friends who found me a chair and kept tourists at bay by suggesting I accepted traveller's cheques, cash, and Diners Cards in any strong currency for my sketches. It worked. I was viewed from a distance, even photographed, but otherwise ignored. Only the challenging bath remained. If I balked at even an impressionistic study, what headaches or what blazing inspiration its seventeenth century creator must have endured, I would guess he spent a lifetime at it.

The bath, set at the centre of a small, extravagantly decorated courtyard, is shaped like a *yoni* with steps leading down from the narrow end. Profusely decorated with three tiers of brilliant stone carving — gods and goddesses mostly and a wealth of floral design — the gilded fountain is an even greater masterpiece. Vishnu and Lakshmi ride a *garuda* which

in turn rests on fishes and crocodiles, turtles and sea monsters. Below the fountain, stone elephants battle. About it four elegantly carved niches stand empty, their images removed by vandals. 'I remember when they were all complete,' volunteered a young shopkeeper who watched me sketch a while. 'The others were here too,' he said, indicating more empty niches and stands, particularly one which must have contained an exquisite gilded image. Only fragments remain.

No water pours from the fountain now, but when it did it was hot and perfumed, suitable for a monarch's pleasure. But I wonder, and no one I have met or nothing I have read stands to correct me, whether the actual procedure of royal bathing in Sundari Chowk was functional or purely ceremonial. I cannot conceive of a king bathing in the open air in Kathmandu's greatly variable climate unless he was obeying the dictates of some ritual, even if the water was hot and his attendants immediately attentive with towels and wraps. Apparently, the whole court looked on while the queen and her ladies watched from behind carved wooden screens. If hearsay is to be believed, the king ascended from his bath to lie on a stone bed where he rested and was massaged with oils. A sign today warns visitors against touching the sacred bed.

Immediately above the gilded fountain is a small stone replica of the famed Krishna temple of Patan. When I wondered aloud why it was there, the obliging shopkeeper said it was because the king who had built the bath was a devotee of Krishna. Indeed he was the very same king who had the Krishna temple built following a dream in which he saw Krishna and Radha making love. Encircling the bath, their heads raised and plumed, are two serpents. Above the steps and looking respectfully into the bath is a vermilioned stone image of Hanuman who was propitiated before every royal dip. And apart from the numerous Hindu and Buddhist deities lining the bath itself there is a vast concourse of carved and painted gods on the buildings all about who observed the royal ablutions.

Until recent times most of Kathmandu valley took its baths at public springs. Though the underground water level has dropped and most springs have consequently run dry, there is a battery of ever-flowing springs in Kathmandu and Patan still immensely popular in all weathers. So perhaps the comparatively private and beautiful Sundari Chowk was the only alternative royalty had to public baths. And Vishnu reincarnate being ritually bathed was surely an occasion of great interest to the court.

Police now guard the courtyard from further desecration. The tourists fill it in relays, endlessly capturing its charms on film. I like to think that some of them will someday look unbelieving at their photographs of a handsome man bathing under a gilded fountain. Lunatic fantasy perhaps, but dreaming comes easily in Sundari Chowk. Every carved and painted piece of wood, every flagstone and every one of its numerous images breathe history. Like the two modern women who strayed unbelievingly into Louis the XV's court at Versailles, someone will someday stumble into a royal Malla occasion. Where better than at the royal bath in Sundari Chowk?

Rape in Eternity Itself

The loveliest women in all of Kathmandu valley are undoubtedly Ganga and Jamuna, two life-size gilded statues that grace a courtyard of the old Malla palace at Patan. They stand as lissomely poised as Bharatnatyam dancers, bejewelled and bare torsoed, their skirts draped about their legs in a manner suggesting movement. Divine dancers. Sister goddesses of mighty rivers that bear their name. Givers of bountiful harvests. The answer to the prayers of a saint of old. Visions of a Newari artist who epitomized all that is beautiful in women. Did he use a model? Was there a woman so exquisite in all the land? No one will ever know. The centuries keep their secrets well, or have carelessly forgotten them. Now the ravages of modern time threaten the very existence of these lovely goddesses who should delight the worshipful and the merely curious for as long as their city endures.

Ganga and Jamuna once wore jewelled headdresses and gilded scarves. They held symbolic objects in their outstretched hands and behind them were screens of fabulously worked metal. There were gems in their belts and necklaces, their armbands and bangles. Their coiled hair was painted and some believe there was colour on their eyes and lips. All this has gone. There remains a suggestion of their golden scarves. Their heads are bare, the objects they held are rembered only by the

spikes that supported them. Ganga, the object of my sketch, has a deep dent above her right knee and metallic bruises where her scarf has been rudely pulled from her shoulder. But still she smiles, resting lightly upon her tortoise, a vision of triumphant beauty.

Ganga and Jamuna stand beside the entrance to a seventeenth century temple to Teleju, the royal goddess. Vandals have stripped the door and its *torana* of almost all their detail. The little which remains gives an idea of how fabulous the originals must have been, a concourse of deities and mythical beasts that somehow failed to guard themselves againt human assault. Somewhere scattered about the globe they give pleasure to those who own them and perhaps tell, in their isolated way, of the glories of the Malla palace at Patan from whence they came. One would wish them back, of course, in the main courtyard called Mul Chowk, where kings of old held court and worshipped. All about are buildings of intricately carved and painted wood. Struts supporting the pagoda roofs depict the many Bhairabs and Matrikas. From latticed windows, ladies of the court watched the proceedings below, and one can still imagine their whisperings and laughter. Do the golden sisters ever speak?

For me, the Mul Chowk at Patan is a sad example of a disease that has swept the world, not only endangering the temples of Nepal but the art of every land. A visitor from England told me of how in the royal chapel of Windsor there are now almost as many guards as tourists, because given half a chance, your blue rinsed lady and your jean clad youth will snap marble fingers or toes from the statues on royal tombs. We were in the Mul Chowk when he said it, and not a guard in sight.

Bamboo scaffolding now creeps across the magnificent façade of Patan's old palace. Foreign and Nepalese experts are helping to restore one of the country's greatest treasures, but short of a miracle they may have arrived too late. True, there are craftsmen in Patan who still can produce great works of art, who can copy with skill and restore with brilliance. But is there a master who can return Ganga and Jamuna to their original magnificence? And sneakingly, I wonder whether they would not look better left as they are: two lovely women who have borne with fortitude the rape of centuries. Two heavenly creatures who remind us of an age when Patan was the city of artists. A city called Eternity Itself.

A Bountiful Rani and a Great Bell

 There are great bells in all the three Durbar Squares of Kathmandu — in Patan, in Bhaktapur and in the capital itself. Wonders of metal casting, I have never discovered whether they were created in situ or as closely nearby, or cast in some foundry somewhere and brought by an army of porters to the spot where they were hung. The latter process sounds too fraught with mishap, and yet since each bell is slung in an elegant frame, it must have been a tremendous labour getting those tons of clanging metal into position. There is one bell, perhaps half as big, that came all the way from England. There, stamped about its mouth for all to see is the legend that it was made in the late nineteenth century in Hull, together with various marks and devices much like those found on good silver spoons.

But these great bells are all Nepalese, cast of several metals, and all about them are inscriptions in old Newari that none of my immediate friends can interpret. The name of the king in whose reign it was cast, surely, and a dedication to the goddess in whose honour it will be rung, but did the people who toiled with wax and clay and metal and fire, who lived with their nerves exposed to the final ordeal lest anything so important and enormous go wrong, did they dare put their humble names upon the bell? I doubt it, but their memory will live forever with the sound they created.

Often it was no ordinary sound that was required of a bell. A king of Bhaktapur one night dreamed he heard the knell of death. It fascinated him. It occupied his waking hours so much that the retelling of his dream became the concern of the court and royal astrologers. A bell, they decided, must be made that would exactly match the sound the king had heard. Imagine the quandary the chosen bell maker found himself in. He could cast a bell yes, and embellish it with all the symbols and emblems of death, but how to ensure it had a sound so abstract as death dreamed by a king.

Sadly, there are no descriptions I know of that tell how this miracle was achieved. What powers were invoked, what secret incantations murmured by Hindu, Buddhist, shaman, tantric or outright witch? What dark potions were flung into the molten metal and with what dread because as surely as they might help to achieve the desired sound, they might crack or blemish the metal. But it was done, and the bell was set up in the Durbar Square beside the Great Bell in Bhaktapur; much smaller, more ornate, but possessed of its singular power. There it remained and every time it was rung the people felt a stab of fear and all the dogs of Bhaktapur howled. In recent times, I can clearly remember it, the Barking Bell, as it came to be known, was removed for repair and never replaced. Perhaps one of its secret contents eventually caused a crack or more probably the city fathers had had enough of howling dogs. Who, after all, even for the fun of it, wants to keep hearing the knell of death?

The great bells were used to sound the time of worship of the goddess Teleju, to raise alarms as and when the city was being attacked, to assemble the people for war, and for less hostile assemblies like royal reviews or proclamations. They are still rung on occasion, but mostly they are secured with iron chains and locks so that children do not ring them all day long.

Bells are everywhere in Kathmandu, in every temple, at every shrine, in the hands of worshipping priests or hung in resonant lines from the eaves of temples to be rung by passing breezes. They are still made for worship, and now also for tourists, small bells mostly in the style of Tibetan lamaist bells that have a thunderbolt for a partner. They have become so popular, they probably ring on tables around the world to summon tea or dinner.

What sets the great Patan bell apart is the statue of a benign Rana maharani which stands in close proximity. Her bronze bust shows brilliantly the court fashions of the day.

Eyebrows pencilled straight across her brows. Eyes heavily outlined. A jewelled head dress with an embroidered veil hanging down her back and a dress heavily encrusted with gold embroidery and gems. There are bows and necklaces, ribbons and orders. A person of striking beauty, her most sublime feature is her hands, gently folded one upon the other, bejewelled and dimpled, the hands of a Mona Lisa in bronze.

I have often admired the statue, on a marble island at the centre of a dirty pond. All about her is a busy market that in its glittery, aggressively feminine way befits her bejewelled highness. I am sure she enjoys the colour and confusion, the sparkling beads, the new plastic, the nose rings and earrings, the bangles and hair ribbons, the bargaining and the squeals of triumph as some humble princess from the hills finds the treasure she has been longing for.

The statue, I had been told, commemorated the maharani's gift to the people of Patan of drinking water of great purity and sweetness. It literally flowed from her hands. But obviously those bountiful days were done. The dirty pond at the base of the maharani's pedestal was far from pure and sweet. So it came as a pleasant, if startling surprise to find, as I sketched the lovely lady, that water suddenly gushed from under her hands, liberally splashing me and my inevitable gathering of interested spectators. 'She always does that,' said a youth knowingly. 'Is it safe to drink?' asked a young girl who merely rinsed her mouth. 'Who is she?' asked someone. 'They say she's a rani of some kind,' said another. Alas! how quickly the years forget even when there are inscriptions in Nepalese and English to enlighten the forgetful:

'Erected by the grateful people of Patan in loving memory of Her Highness the late Bara Maharani who, jointly with her husband, Major General Maharaja Chandra Sumshere Jung Bahadur Rana CCSI.'

A Temple to a Compassionate God

One of Patan's most famous and handsome temples is dedicated to the red god Machhendranath or Avilokiteswara Padmapani. Legend places its origin centuries ago, but it is recorded as having been constructed in 1673, probably over a much older shrine. Its three pagoda roofs are made of gilded metal, golden serpents coil about its high finial and its two tiers of beautifully carved wooden struts depict manifestations of Avilokiteswara, and the torments of the damned in hell. The doorways are particularly beautiful, each a masterpiece of high renaissance Newari carving, and each guarded by stone lions.

Beautiful as the temple is, it pales before the legends that surround it. Rato or Red Machhendranath is saint and god both, Karunamaya the compassionate and merciful one; Padmapani, the fourth of the five Buddhas of the elements, Lokeswar. There was a time when Shiva was his guru, learning from him the secret of being one with the Supreme Being. A charming story tells of how Parvati once struggled to keep awake while Shiva recounted to her all that he had learned from Lokeswar. Lokeswar himself, eager to listen, assumed the guise of a fish. Somehow Shiva came to know that he was being overheard and threatened to put a curse upon the eavesdropper. Lokeswar immediately appeared before a repentant Shiva and Parvati and was ever since known as Machhendranath, from the word *machha* for fish.

But what bestows particular importance upon the god to the people of the Kathmandu valley is the tale of how he came to the valley and has remained to this day. There was a time beyond the reach of memory when a great twelve-year drought brought terrible suffering and death to the valley of Kathmandu. Fields and forests scorched where they stood. The earth cracked and powdered. There was no water in river or tank or spring. When it seemed there was no end to this terrible visitation, the king's religious advisers, after months of prayer and soul-searching, divined that the fault lay with the great sage Gorakhnath who, by sitting in meditation over the holes of the snake gods giving rain, had prevented their normal activities. The snakes were not only trapped but angered. So also apparently was Gorakhnath who felt slighted that the people of the valley hadn't shown him sufficient respect. He planned the drought as a punishment.

Now one didn't go about interfering with great saints in meditation, so a way had to be devised to get Gorakhnath to move himself without anger and embarrassment all around. There was but one way and that was to persuade Machhendranath, who was a guru of Gorakhnath, to come to Kathmandu so that the meditating saint would rise to greet him. Trouble was, Machhendranath himself was away in Assam, meditating. Neither could Gorakhnath be persuaded to interrupt his guru's meditation by journeying to Assam to meet him, just as there was no hope of Gorakhnath being moved without bringing Machhendranath to him in Kathmandu.

Of one thing the royal Nepalese astrologers and priests were certain. If the compassionate Machhendranath heard of

the plight of the people of Kathmandu he would surely come to the valley forthwith. So the king of Bhaktapur, a learned tantric from Kathmandu and a farmer from Patan set off for Assam, resolved to bring Machhendranath to their valley.

Good fortune had the snake god, Karkot Naga, join them along the way. He had a way with obstructing demons that firmly trounced them. But his powers failed before Machhendranath's mother who was determined not to let her son leave Assam. Here the Patan tantric came into his own.

He cast such powerful spells that Machhendranath, despite every device known to his mother, transformed himself into a large black bumblebee and flew into a golden casket that the tantric had brought for the purpose. Demons captured the casket and all seemed lost until the Patan tantric invoked the four ferocious Bhairabs, most terrifying of gods, to aid them. The demons fled, happily leaving the golden casket behind them, and the road to Kathmandu lay open.

Arriving in the Kathmandu valley, the weary party stopped to rest at a spot two miles from Patan. As predicted, no sooner had the news reached Gorakhnath than he rose from his meditation and hurried to meet his guru. The snake gods were released. Rain fell in torrents, the valley bloomed, and people rejoiced. At about the same time Bhairab came to visit Machhendranath and was heard to bark out the sound *Bu* which is the Newari word for birthplace. Hearing this, the king ordered a town to be built on the spot, to be known as Bungamati, and here the golden casket containing Machhendranath, still in the form of a bumblebee, was enshrined. The king further made lavish land endowments for the maintenance of the temple and appointed priests to worship Machhendranath as the god of rain and harvests.

A peculiarity of Machhendranath is that he is considered male and female both; father and mother whose religious rites are both male and female in their performance. There is also confusion about Minanath, a deity associated with Machhendranath, considered variously to be his son or daughter. A priest at the temple of Minanath, however, reacted violently to this belief. Minanath, he assured me was much older than Machhendranath, so the question didn't arise.

Whatever the legends, and they are as numerous as they are wondrous, the god who over the centuries has assumed the form of a red-faced image with downcast, benevolent eyes, spends time both at Bungamati, his birthplace, and Patan, where his beautiful temple stands in a large, uncluttered courtyard. Once a year he is taken in slow, majestic procession, enshrined in a *rath* with massive wooden wheels representing the four terrifying Bhairabs, and a long wooden yoke with a gilded mask that represents Karkot, the snake god. A tall spire of bamboo, greenery and flowers tops the chariot and has to be kept in place with restraining ropes. It is amazing that so huge and clumsy a construction moves at all, but it progresses slowly through the streets and squares of Patan while everyone, of every faith and rank from the king to his humblest subject, comes to pay respect to the god.

At one stage of the cumbersome journey, Machhendranath visits his mother, who manifest as a tree, stands in a small square about which his chariot is respectfully drawn three times.

Finally, at a culminating festival the jewelled waistcoat of the god, which again, is the subject of much colourful legend, is shown to the crowd. The king and queen and all high-ranking government officials and military officers are present, as is the Kumari of Patan.

It is customary for rain to fall on this day and many are the observers of the Nepalese scene who over the centuries have advised that it is unwise to venture out on the waistcoat viewing day without raincoat or umbrella. I can testify to being rained upon.

A Victim of the Mahabharata

 In the heart of Kathmandu, where streets old and new meet in a small square known as Indra Chowk, is a temple of uncertain date dedicated to Akash Bhairab, or the Bhairab of the sky. The present structure, but for its powerful embellishments, is much like an old Nepalese house; tiled, two storied, with a row of shops on the ground floor. The square is a meeting place for just about everybody, from Kathmandu, the surrounding valley and the distant mountains, and well-known to visitors from India who pass it in their perambulations between the modern shops and supermarket and the small but enticing shops in the old Asan bazaar where Tibetan traders sell goodies from Bangkok and Hong Kong.

Until recently, the two handsome metal lions on either side of the entrance door used to provide convenient display for a fruit vendor who innocently hung bunches of bananas from the gaping jaws or tied a shading umbrella to the mane or tail. She has been tidied up and in the effort has deprived tourists of a splendid photograph. But rickshaws and *thelas,* happy porters from the hills and tentative pavement shops that bloom between the coming and going of policemen, lend a busy charm to Indra Chowk. Within reach are a shimmering bead market, shops selling *pashmina* shawls of every quality, fruit and flower vendors, and flute men. These unsung musicians,

some of them quite brilliant, stand under trees made of flutes stuck into bamboo poles enticing passers-by with the latest Hindi film song or the most popular tunes of Radio Nepal.

The actual shrine is on the first floor, at its centre a large silver mask of God Bhairab stained with the vermilion and yellow of endless anointing. Always there are flowers and usually the much beloved marigold. The eyes of the god are turned upward giving emphasis to the incredible story connected with the deity.

It is told that the first Kiranti king, a great warrior, by the name of Yalambar was anxious to take part in the epic war of the Mahabharata then being fought on the plains of India. He went suitably attired in the armour of the times and upon his face wore a dazzling silver mask representing Bhairab, Lord of Terror. And with him went a seemingly invincible horde of Nepalese warriors. One can imagine his appearance on the battlefield; a mighty figure at the head of a terrifying army even among the warring gods and epic mortals about him. Indeed, so powerful was his presence that Lord Krishna appeared before him to ask whose side the king and his army had come to join. Yalambar grandly said that he would ally himself to the losing forces. Whereupon, Krishna fearing that Yalambar would join the Kauravas, decapitated the king with a blow so powerful that his masked head flew across the lower ranges of the Himalayas to come to rest in Kathmandu.

There is another version of this story which has the beheaded Yalambar beg of Krishna that his eyes be permitted to view the battle until its end. Many versions of the ancient books, the *Puranas*, record that this heroic request was granted and only when the war ceased did Yalambar's head return to Kathmandu. The existing temple in the old bazaar fails in its humble way to match so stupendous an act, so immortal a deed. True, the windows through which the image can be glimpsed are beautifully carved and four large gilded gryphons, outside the windows, appear to be hurling themselves into the sky. There are rows of prayer lamps along the balcony of the first floor and the façade is tricked out with a variety of porcelain tiles, which at a glance appear incongruous but grow on one so that it is difficult to imagine the temple, placed as it is at the meeting place of old and new Kathmandu to be any different.

Once a year at the time of the Kumari Jatra which coincides with Indra Jatra, the great silver mask of the Akash Bhairab is enthroned in the square below the temple. Thousands come to worship and feed the god so that his silver face almost disappears beneath countless garlands and bouquets and votive offerings.

Aptly, the mask of the Akash Bhairab has been adopted as the symbol of Nepal's flag carrier — Royal Nepal Airlines. And I like to think that the god is pleased that his epic journey is commemorated every day by the Kathmandu-Delhi-Kathmandu flight.

A Temple to a Secretive Goddess

 Patan's temple to Balkumari is beautifully located on the outskirts of the town. The city hasn't reached it yet, and the track that leads to it, a country lane, is uneven, dusty, and flanked by wild hedgegrows. Great old trees tower above the building on one side, shading it in summer, and in winter providing a screen of filigree through which rolling countryside, village, the valley wall and high snow summits can be seen. In days gone by it must have been a lonely, isolated spot, probably forested, a place where travellers halted briefly and made offerings for a journey begun or ended. A temple grew.

The *pujari* of the temple told me that the original image was of stone. Then, presumably miraculously it supported images of Balkumari on one side and Bhairab on the other: it's still there, in a small pit below the more recent metal image. I asked him if it was true that Balkumari was a consort of Bhairab, or a female manifestation of the god of terror. He answered that she was married but her husband's identity was a closely kept secret. He knew of course, but he must never divulge the information. The goddess' husband is just one of the mysteries surrounding the goddess. Apparently, she is deeply shrouded in them, mysteries that the temple priests alone see in rare visions. At least one of my books, which to

a page are strangely silent or hesitant about the Patan Balkumari, do say she is one of Bhairab's many consorts but the *pujari* greeted this information with a look of exasperation and a fairly rude noise.

Why, I asked him, did the exquisite gilded image of her in the temple represent her riding a peacock? Why was there a peacock on a high stone pedestal facing the temple? That apparently was a fairly modern interpretation. She was originally a stone goddess; presumably, though he refused to say it, one of the early mother goddesses. Then why Bal? If she was a mother goddess, with a secret, powerful consort, why was she represented as a girl? My Nepalese friends and I were obviously trespassing upon the mysteries. The *pujari* wore a beatific smile which could have been one of long suffering.

'She has sisters,' he volunteered. 'Younger sisters. Mahalaxmi and Sikhabhai.' An intelligent young man standing nearby suggested that Balkumari was one of the *ashtamatrikas,* but the *pujari* snorted again. Her companions in the temple are Ganesh, Bhairab, Dakshin Kali, Mahalaxmi and Bhairabi. Asked their significance, the *pujari* gathered himself up and walked away. 'She is a goddess of sickness,' said the intelligent young man. 'Her powers are particularly efficacious in the treatment of dysentry and diarrhoea. People who worship her and live under her influence seldom suffer these diseases. She is also propitiated by the newly married and young men straight from their thread ceremonies.'

To sketch the early seventeenth century temple, sat in a small sunken courtyard, its four approaches guarded by large stone lions, I climbed atop a nearby building where interference from passers-by was minimal. One of the inevitable old men who crouch about temples either as their official or unofficial guardians asked my driver what the American was doing. Had he perhaps come to steal the image? Apparently his suspicions are well founded, though why he got them confused with Americans I can't think. There are three Bal Kumari images in Patan. The main one is in the temple of my sketch, another is in a prayer house that once belonged to a Malla king, and the third is in a potters' colony. The latter has remained untouched. The one from the Malla prayer house has been stolen and recovered twice. The temple deity has also been stolen twice but never recovered: the present image, of a lovely woman riding a peacock, her head slightly inclined, her slender hands in a prayerful *mudra* is the second replica. The handsome Ganesh image that stands besides it is also comparatively new, the original having been stolen.

As I sketched the temple, a small procession arrived carrying a gilded image of Balkumari that looked exactly like the one in the shrine. It was dumped without much ceremony against a pillar, where passers-by, mostly women, paid obeisance, or children tinkled the small bells that are part of the image.

The image has been stolen several times. The first time it was stolen it was recovered from the customs before it could leave the country. A devotee from Patan who happened to be there at the time instantly recognized the goddess. Strangely, the image is light enough for a single priest to carry easily. Yet, in its box in the customs shed it had assumed magical weight.

The second time this lovely image was stolen it disappeared for a year. When the three persons responsible for stealing it fell out over its disposal, the police got to know and it was found in a private house buried in the floor. Legend or coincidence; as the image was uncovered, Patan was rocked by an earthquake. Perhaps divine intervention also prevented the beautiful gilded finial being stolen quite recently. A sudden high wind unseated the thief as he dislodged his golden prize from the temple roof so that he fell with an alarming clatter and broke his leg in the bargain. Easily caught, he was bound to a post supporting the temple bell and given a sound beating. Ah yes, the finial he attempted to steal was not the original. That had been stolen ages before.

The moral behind the story of this lovely temple in sylvan surroundings, is surely that treasures should not be kept in temptingly isolated places. Not in today's crass world of image lifters.

Patan's Grand Temple Golden

 I've been funking this sketch for ages, ever since I turned my attention to the lovely city of Patan. I've been visiting the Golden Temple once or twice a week. Searching for possible angles. Examining its myriad details. Shrinking from tides of tourists even as I summoned up enough courage to begin. Making excuses of too little or too much light, freezing temperatures and sneaky breezes. There is a Nepalese saying, even more expressive than *domane* or *manyana,* which merely puts off for tomorrow what could be done today. *Bholi parsi* is tomorrow or the day after, and if tomorrow sometimes comes, *parsi* certainly doesn't. I've been *bholi parsiying* like mad over the fabulous Golden Temple which is no single masterpiece, rather a collection of masterpieces, big and small, fused into a shrine of overwhelming grandeur.

There is the extravagance of gold that lands the first punch: gold from ground level to high finials. Golden roofs, golden images, golden friezes of intricate detail, golden birds perched on upturned, golden eaves. Golden serpents. Rearing golden griffins, and delicate golden parasols shading the highest finials. It takes time to get the whole extraordinary thing into focus, to grasp the magnificent concept, appreciate the proportions, the use of space, to isolate detail. Above one's head, for instance, as one stands in amazement at the entrance,

is a frieze of deities and mythical beasts. The artistry is stunning. Two divine beings, long deprived of the stringed instruments they played, have hands so exquisitely fashioned that they form sound the way *mudras* speak. Their hands are no bigger than a thumb nail. At the same spot, just before one, are twin tableaux of gilded princes riding gilded elephants, stood on gilded tortoises, as high as a tall man.

The actual temple reaches across one side of a small courtyard. At the centre of the courtyard is a much smaller shrine, a *chaitya,* more golden than the temple itself. Under its eaves, and facing the main door of the temple, are seried ranks of royal images; kings and queens in ancient stone and gilded metal who, in search of immortality, left their likenesses behind. Two of them, though only to be guessed at, are the legendary Marwari queen, Pingala, and her unknown husband, who are believed to have built the temple. By way of legends no one knows when, but temple records reach back to 1409 when the gilded *kalash* was installed on the finial.

So lavish a display of devotion must have had special reason, which has one wondering why this spot is so hallowed, why such largesse was poured upon it. The other great temples of Kathmandu valley commemorate miracles: the appearance of Shiva in an incinerating light; the settling of a divine lotus when the lake on which it floated was drained by a slash of a deity's sword; the coming of the royal goddess. Ancient Patan was largely a Buddhist city. It is believed that Gautam Buddha visited it and stayed a while. Close to the Golden Temple is a small courtyard where the Buddha baptised a king and gave to a caste of metalworkers his own name. It could be possible that this glorious temple was built upon miraculous foundations, perhaps upon the very spot where the Buddha was supposed to have dwelt. But even legend has lost its memory.

Were archaeologists to burrow into a mound nearby that locals point out as an ancient palace, they might find an answer. From the mound, upon which the inevitable peepal tree holds together a mute profusion of crumbling brick and stone, it is possible to guess at the old city. The Malla palace with its filigreed courtyards, temples, baths and statuary is a reach away. Passing below the mound is the highway from Kathmandu, the old trade route between India and Tibet. Set beside it is the glitter of the Golden Temple, the first great monument, other than an Ashoka stupa the traveller from the north would have happened upon. Before the city grew about the temple, it must have been surrounded by the houses of priests and devotees. There is even a suggestion at the main outer gate that the shrine might have been walled about: there remains a small corridor of heavy, chiselled stone reminiscent of the forts of distant Rajasthan. Today's walls are made by two floors of building, and one is occupied by a monastery.

Following ancient custom, the people attached to the monastery, which means nearby shopkeepers, businessmen, and the likes of such new breeds as office workers and mechanics, take their turn at serving the temple. Men, their heads shaved and wearing white, perform religious rites and adhere to a strict convention of rules during the month they serve. So I have found the jolly young curio dealer with whom I have spent much time haggling over prices and who is something of a Honda-riding Romeo, suddenly shorn and barefooted, padding about the temple courtyard with all the dignity he can command. Another, who has done his month of service, tells me why the exquisite silver doors of the temple are now guarded by unlovely wrought iron barricades and why the once mobile image of the Buddha has been riveted to its base: image lifters, who think nothing of scaling the surrounding buildings and coming over the roofs at night. Few thieves anywhere could find themselves in such tempting surroundings.

I have yet to visit the temple at three o'clock in the morning when the day's *pujas* begin. My friends about the temple tell me it is an experience not to be missed, a time when magic is afoot, when the gods are very close and even temple thieves relent.

A Temple to Ravana's Memory

 The original shrine was larger, more garishly muralled. A painted face as large as the building. Two staring eyes, a grimacing mouth, coiling serpents and a string of human heads pouring blood. At the base of the mural, and at its exact centre, was a small altar into which was set an earthen pot filled with fine branches and bamboos. The painting, done in shocking red, yellow, white and black was discoloured at its centre with the blood of many sacrifices. As I painted it, people passing along a nearby track came to touch their hands or foreheads to the pot. When some men arrived with a buffalo for sacrifice and began their *pujas,* I packed up my material and fled. I remember the shed-like building stood in a river bed, beside some towering rocks beautifully sculpted by water over the centuries. The main stream flowed close by, and just upriver from the temple was a bridge made of several heavy logs. A quiet place. A lovely valley with forests capping the surrounding mountain tops. But even in the remotest of places, people gather to watch something so unusual as a large, foreign gentleman sitting on a rock painting. The children come first. After a while they start calling shrilly to parents or relatives in nearby farmhouses, particularly if the houses or people figured in the sketch.

'Quickly, come quickly. He's just done a drawing of auntie Shanti.' And then inevitably follow the words I have yet to distinguish from each other, *'bala'* and *'bamla.' Bala* means good and *bamla,* as might well be imagined, means bad. It is an unnerving experience sitting in a crowd of children chanting words suggestively awful. By the time the elders have arrived to give their expert opinion on the sketch or painting, *balas* and *bamlas* fairly come to blows. Which is time to call a halt and ask questions. I was lucky to have the *pujari* of the temple in the crowd. Apart from objecting to the omission of some gore in the top left hand corner, he announced me *bala* and readily answered my questions.

The track that passes the temple and arches across the river, was the old highway between Kathmandu and the plains of India. Along it passed pilgrims and sages, demons and gods. The pilgrims were plagued by spirits infesting the valley and so various shrines had been built at the spot to give them spiritual courage. Invariably, the rising river water, which in truth was the spirits, washed these shrines away. When, during the time of the Rana prime ministers it was attempted to build a proper road along the track, an army of spirits, witches and demons thwarted the attempt. The road was abandoned.

But this particular shrine was very old. It commemorated the passing and brief halt of Ravana at the spot as he returned to Sri Lanka from the Himalayas, where he had gone to ask a boon of Shiva. Shiva gave him a pot of mountain water to take with him, with the warning that it must never be placed on the ground. The jubilant Ravana got as far as Tikka Bhairab, to give the spot its name, without mishap, but was suddenly siezed with something akin to the Kathmandu belly. Looking frantically about, he saw a cowherd and entreated him to hold the pot most carefully. Finding it much too heavy to hold while Ravana disappeared behind some bushes, the cowherd placed it on a rock and made off with the speed of terror. One can imagine the collective rage on all those many faces when Ravana found his instructions abused. Drawing his mighty sword, he struck at the offending rock with all his might so that it split down the centre and the pot settled in the cleft. Why Ravana then went off in a demonic huff leaving his boon behind, the *pujari* couldn't explain. 'Perhaps he wanted to leave it here,' suggested an elder who thought my sketch was *bala*. 'He knew it would be looked after and worshipped.'

When I returned to Tikka Bhairab to do my sketch, I found a completely new building and mural, and the large, lonely pine that shaded it has quite disappeared. The children collected and the elders came, and a dear old woman told me sorrowfully that a great flood had washed not only the tree and the temple away, but the small bazaar including her house as well. Perhaps the spirits had been enraged for some inexplicable reason. They may not have liked the new mural, for every year the same family of artists from Patan comes to renew the painting, and from a comparison of photographs and my own sketches, their inspiration differs from year to year. This year the demon's face is smaller and he wears a crown, rather than a necklace, of human heads. The old shingle roof has been replaced by corrugated aluminum sheeting, and the whole building has been raised a few more feet above the river level. Half of the stone that Ravana cut is still there. The other has been shattered by the fury of the water. There remains the pot set in its low altar, but whether it is the same one is doubtful.

How was it that a temple associated with Ravana became dedicated to Bhairab? It seems that when a high-powered party from the Kathmandu valley went to Assam centuries ago to coax the god Machhendranath to take up residence in Nepal, they travelled this way. They were protected by four fierce Bhairabs against a pursuit of angry demons. One of the Bhairabs decided to stay at this lovely and strategic river crossing to guard the escape route. It is his bold likeliness that is painted on the wall of the shrine. His silver mask, that adorns the pot of river water, stands on the low sacrificial altar. And it is to him that countless sacrifices are made. Interesting to remember is the fact that Bhairab is the most ferocious manifestation of Shiva, and it was Shiva's pot of water that Ravana left at Tikka Bhairab. For god and demon both, the spot is *bala*.

The Village of the Dancing Durga

Thecho, sat astride the old trade route to India, wears a well-to-do-look of prosperous farmers living in prosperous houses but conservative enough to have so far shunned concrete. The stout brick houses that line each side of the road are built one against the other, their windows carved of wood, their eaves hung with garlands of vegetables and chillies. The buildings stand respectfully back from the road, or perhaps they keep the bustle and dust at arm's length. But no Newari farmer will waste good land, so between road and houses are a continuous line of small temples and shrines, mostly Buddhist. There are some incredibly filthy water tanks in which women wash clothes and cooking utensils that look remarkably clean after the ordeal. I asked my driver if his wife used the likes of these village ponds to wash his belongings. He replied abruptly that he would beat her up. Sheep, dogs, fowl, and duck weave their way through knots of people idly sunning themselves outside their front doors. Women naked to the waist, oil themselves and their new born infants as they take in the sun and leave it to elder relatives to hoosh cameramen away.

Thecho was founded in the sixteenth century by a Malla king of nearby Patan who designed it as a convenient shield for his city. At first, stout farmers resisted invaders or gangs

of dacoits using the road from India. But it was not long before
the village, almost large enough to be a town, prospered and
developed a character of its own. How it began no one knows
and even legends are at variance, but Thecho became
renowned for its dance troupe. At one of their earliest
performances, a great tantric sage caused the many
manifestations of the goddess Durga to possess the dancers.
Imagine the scene. Lithe masked bodies suddenly charged with
the awesome majesty of the mighty goddess. Human arms

multiplying, papier mâché masks becoming divine faces, tinsel costumes transformed to the raiment of heaven.

Then leaping and swirling, these bodies possessed, danced through the fields to Patan and the very palace itself. The king, a great patron of the dance, was so awed, so deeply moved, he invited the dancers into the most sacred courtyard of the palace and there for one holy, unforgettable night the goddesses danced. Ever after, the dancers of Thecho perform once a year at Dashain in the Mul Chowk of Patan's old palace.

In search of these famous dancers, I was unexpectedly shown into a house which I had been told was closed to all visitors. We mounted a narrow dark stairway and entered a room heavy with the scent of incense, wax, decay and damp. There, by guttering candlelight, I was shown a collection of masks hung on a smoke-blackened wall. They were smeared with saffron and vermilion and I believed blood, and imagination-on-edge gave them life, so that sightless eyes and painted mouths looked stern, pathetically sad, angry, demanding and lustful. The goriest was the mask of Durga herself, like a decapitated head washed in its own blood, its eyes still seeing, its mouth gaping open. An old drum hung from the rafters. I was told it was the drum of the death of ten generations. When I asked what exactly that meant, my question hung unanswered as if my informant had been mesmerized. But after a while he told me in a harsh whisper that the dancers who wear these masks become so possessed by the goddesses they represent, they drink the blood of sacrificial animals. Once in ages past, they consumed the blood of human sacrifice.

Was it then that the drum sounded? The women of Thecho apparently still threaten their children by saying that the Nava Durga will get them if they are naughty.

Near the temple of the Nava Durga is a dilapidated oil press filled with a luminous gloom and the smell of freshly ground mustard. The machinery is primitive and much of it I suspect, once belonged to an antiquated car whose shell still hangs in a corner. The press once belonged to a single family but is now owned by a commune. Thecho today has some twenty oil presses and oil goes mostly to Patan. So mustard oil, pressed from the gloriously yellow fields that reach in terraces about the village, replaces the riches that once flowed up and down the old trade route. And there are, of course, the dancers.

The Water Gardens of Balaju

 When I first came upon the gardens some thirty years ago, they snuggled naturally into the mountain side they were built upon. Clear water tanks fed from mountain springs were full of carp, some so large they must have been there for years. They glided about in the most subtle of greys, greens, blues and silver, rising in splashing excitement to be fed by visitors. At the time of the bathing festival in April, when the area is crowded with vividly dressed pilgrims, the fish gormandise. But they alone do not make Balaju. The gardens, built by a Malla king who apparently craved peace and solitude, are famous for their twenty-two carved stone fountains, that stand in a line below the tanks, emptying themselves into a long, shallow bathing pool. The central fountain is enormous and bathers battle the force of its gushing water. All are carved to resemble water monsters with curled trunks, staring eyes, ferocious teeth and tongues aflame. It is explained that the sculptor responsible for these handsome water spouts had never seen the crocodiles he endeavoured to portray; an amusing story that dismisses an artist's creativity too glibly.

I can remember lawns as natural as forest clearings, and a pilgrim's rest house hidden behind willow trees. Also, a small sacred tank, untouched, in which a large stone image of Vishnu reclines on a bed of snakes. It is a fairly faithful replica

of the great Lichhavi image at Buddhanilkantha, north of the gardens, but lacks the serenity and perfect proportions of the original. It is said that a Malla king had water channelled from the sacred pool at Buddhanilkantha to the palace in Kathmandu. On the very night that the water splashed into a palace pool, the monarch had a dream in which Vishnu of the blue throat appeared to him. The god warned that not only the king but his descendants would die if ever they went to see the reclining image at Buddhanilkantha. So the king had a replica of the image made and installed with due ceremony at Balaju. Here the kings of Nepal may worship without fear, for it is generally believed that were the king to die as a result of looking upon the Buddhanilkantha image, great and terrifying would be the misfortunes that would befall the kingdom.

Today this garden carved from the forests that cover the sacred mountain of Nagarjun, has been landscaped with an elaborate use of concrete. There are flower beds and pools shaped like fish and clubs and diamonds and spades and hearts. Usually the new pools are stagnant and their fountains refuse to play. The flower beds try valiantly to battle the press of people. At one corner of the gardens is a modern swimming pool which is a source of great pleasure to locals and visitors. I am being romantic and outdated, I know, but I love the natural levels of the old gardens, the forests all about and the trees full of birdsong. It hardly matters. Balaju is essentially a place of pilgrimage, and pilgrims and Saturday bathers have their ablutions firmly in mind. Beauty is secondary.

The whole of the Balaju area is sacred. The mountain Nagarjun that rises in great folds about it is associated with the Buddha. It seems that when he visited Nepal and intended to journey into Tibet, the forces of evil in that country were so strong the Buddha was advised not to go. Instead, he climbed the Nagarjun hill from where, facing the great barrier of mountains that separate Nepal from Tibet, he delivered a sermon to the Tibetan people. As a result, it is a spot of deep significance to Tibetan Buddhists who have erected a stupa on the summit of the mountain. Close by also is the sacred hill of Mhaipi from which clay was taken to build the temple of Machhendranath in Patan. It is known to be the abode of powerful witches and spirits who had to be subdued by tantric priests before the earth could be removed. And just across a shallow river from Balaju is the hill top retreat of Guru Nanak, the great saint of Sikhism, who cured a Nepalese monarch of unsound mind before disappearing into Tibet.

None of these considerations prevented Balaju from becoming a modern industrial area, where almost everything is manufactured from silk and watches to Coca-Cola. The town spreads alarmingly below Nagarjun but stops short at the forest wall. The trees and the still comforting peace of gardens will surely remain. There are still fat carp in the water tanks, sailing idly through the clear water. And though some of the fountains threaten to run dry, there will always be pilgrims and weekend bathers to use them.

If only the modern fountains would play.

The Pottery Temple

The temple itself is distinctly ordinary. But for its tiled Nepalese porch supported on carved wooden pillars, it might be a mausoleum, squat, white plastered and topped by a squashed dome, beloved of pigeons. But the tall ascending plinths point to better things and grander times when in all probability the temple was a proud Newari structure of bricks and carved wood with gilded roofs. It was built by the powerful prime minister of a famous king, Pratap Malla, when the trade route between Tibet and India passed within yards of it. Toppled by an earthquake that spared only its plinths and stone images — a Shivalingam and a complete set of panchayana deities — the original temple was replaced by the present uninspired structure in testimony of the decline of Newari sculpture and a passing interest in Moghul styles.

What makes the temple immediately fascinating is the pottery piled about it; a small mountain of urns, bowls, flowerpots, and terracotta animals of every size that hide the plinths and make the temple at the top the largest confection of them all. Just when the city's dealers in pottery took over the temple, no one appears to know. The kindly gentleman who offered me a hastily cleaned stool on which to sit to sketch, and who literally thumped inquisitive children out of my way, said long, long ago with an inflection which in

Nepalese indicates great. Great age, great size, great distance, great anything. Perhaps his ancestors came when the temple was first built, I said, and he replied may be, I think to please me. Since the populous city of Kathmandu must have required pottery for a thousand uses long before the temple was built, perhaps the dealers in pots predated it.

It doesn't matter. What does, is that this marvellously attractive exhibition of Nepalese pottery exists, in one place, in the centre of old Kathmandu. Some of the shapes never change. The large, proud water and rice jars were probably shaped centuries ago and were decorated with the same bold patterns of deep red clay that adorn them still. Unless distilling methods have radically changed over the years, the fat, round

The Pottery Temple / **161**

pots with perforations at their base were used when King Pratap Malla ruled in the seventeenth century. Certainly the cleanly proportioned bowls in which clothes are washed or out of which cattle drink, must have been fashioned by the earliest potters. But when did the elephants creep in, their backs and heads hollowed to receive plants or bulbs? They are the first of the animal pots I remember, jumbos with trunks curled between their front legs or raised in salute that look stunningly attractive when they carry vast loads of cacti, bulbs, flowering plants and ferns. So irresistible is their appeal that they can be seen being hefted aboard departing aeroplanes with the kind of affection bestowed on favourite ailing aunts. Several thousands are even now at the International Garden Fair in Munich, where one hopes they will battle with all those gnomes and seven dwarfs for supremacy.

Now there are horses, lions, griffins, rhino, duck and peacock vying with the elephants, even gnomes, yes even gnomes which one can only suspect are an offshoot of foreign aid. Creativity has gone further by translating famous landmarks to pottery, so that there are Bhim Sen minarets among the flower pots, and temples of five stages. One day, some turned-on potter might be moved to produce a Sheraton Hotel or a Chinese trolley bus. What the rummager can find on and about the plinths of the Naudega temple are beautiful wall plaques depicting gods and angels and an all-time favourite in danger of becoming extinct, a Victorian lady who I suspect was once a Rana maharani.

The high plinths of the Naudega temple also support families of Indian haircutters who ply their trade from under ancient umbrellas. They take over immediately where the pottery ends so that some of their customers are afforded the comfort of a pottery back rest. And where the haircutters end are the *thwang-thwang* men, those gentlemen carrying strange harp-like instruments who invariably have white cotton fluff adhering to their hair, *lungis* and vests. They congregate around nearby shops selling cotton of various grades and will beat and tease as much of the stuff you buy, while Muslim tailors run up mattresses, *razais* and pillows from cloth bought from the Dumbarkumari shops next door.

Dumbarkumari is Indian muslin hand printed in bold red, black and orange designs by Muslim printers near the great Hindu shrine of Pashupatinath. Its name apparently immortalizes the daughter of the first Rana prime minister, Jung Bahadur, who was greatly enamoured by the cloth. Though Indian in origin, Dumbarkumari is as Nepalese as it can get and is worn, slept under and over and wrapped about by just about everyone.

There are the occasional auctioneers who use the plinths of the temple as their stage. Anyone interested in an old piano without its innards? The discarded sets for a religious drama? A suite of old furniture minus springs but home to a family of rats? Tins, bottles, packing cases, machinery that might once have been a car?

If the powerful prime minister was to see the temple now, he might be dismayed by the lacklustre building that replaced his original creation. But surely he would be interested and not a little amused by the goings-on about it.

The Vanishing Courtyard of the Medicine Men

 To begin at a not very distant beginning. Seven years ago the courtyard or *bahal* was the loveliest in Kathmandu, its four sides of mellow, unpointed brick decorated with brilliantly carved wooden windows and arched verandahs, a masterpiece of Newari architecture in desperate need of preservation. For, already there were signs of decay, the most serious being the disintegration of the family. I never discovered how many sons, or may be brothers, had inherited the building, but the division began to show immediately. A section of one side of the courtyard was being permitted to crack and crumble. The woodwork was splintering under the pressures of collapse: a window being forced from its brick seating, a carved verandah post tilting crazily outward. Expressing concern that I realized was none of my business, I was told that the damage would soon be repaired. Had I not noticed a metal plaque embossed with the figure of a flute playing Krishna in the wall where the most ominous crack had developed? It indicated a temple to Krishna which would never be permitted to fall, even if the rest did. The rest has fallen and is now a mound of mud and bricks and shattered wood. The Krishna temple just stands, but apparently its deities have been removed to some safer shrine.

Where, I asked some children, who gathered about me as I sketched, had the lovely windows of the collapsed building gone? I remembered they comprised birds and mythical beasts with *jaalis* inspired by dancing peacocks. 'They took them,' an elder girl said, conjuring up visions of shadowy people scattering in a night what it had taken superb artists years to create. 'We took the birds to play with.'

Ironically, none or all of this is anybody's fault. Since I first came to Kathmandu and saw the old city rushing to give way to a new, modern capital, I happened upon the perfectly sound argument put forward by those who live in exquisite old houses, that they have both the right and desire to change. It goes like this. We know you foreigners feel strongly about it, but would you like to live with little or no light and air coming through your carved windows, with ceilings so low you can hardly stand upright, with stairs so steep and dark they are a perpetual menace and with little or no sanitation whatsoever? We desire modern homes with modern amenities. We do, after all, live in the twentieth century, not during the Newari renaissance of the fifteenth and seventeenth centuries.

Over to the government and to all those foreign agencies bent upon preservation and restoration. There is just so much they can do. With every corner of the Kathmandu valley a veritable museum, there is a limit to what can and cannot be protected. There is also, unfortunately, a limit to bureaucracy's interest and perseverance, whether of the local, foreign or interbred variety. While experts ponder feasibility reports and meet in endless consultation, treasures of immeasurable worth crumble and disappear. Like the beautiful courtyard of the medicine men in Kathmandu where kings may have come to consult or royal potions were brewed; where travellers from distant India and Tibet came for panaceas for their many ills and where secrets, many centuries old, were distilled and recorded in guarded minds. Or, like the fabulous wooden window in Bhaktapur that had incorporated in its carved design the proof of distant travel along the Silk Road — the ungainly camel. It was promised restoration by a foreign agency. A gentleman on the certain collapse of the building, asked if I was interested in buying some wood carving. I obviously disappointed him by saying the building should be restored and all its carving and statuary kept carefully to that end. The courtyard no longer belongs to one person, he explained. Some liked it as it was. Some didn't and were affecting changes as I could see from a battery of modern windows that had replaced the old in one corner of the courtyard. Probably the family who owned the badly damaged part were waiting for it to fall before either building anew or selling the property. Either way it was doomed. Already the courtyard was blemished beyond repair. I should think about his offer, said the old man. And he was gone.

The Krishna plaque remains. 'If anyone touches that,' said one of the children crowded about me, 'they will die of bleeding from the nose and mouth. It will be very terrible. They will turn thin like skeletons and become evil ghosts.' Who had put such a curse on the plaque, I asked, but she wasn't sure. Someone long long ago, much older than her grandfather who had already celebrated his seventy-seventh birthday. What a sadness that a similar curse had not been put on the entire building so that its wooden traceries, its carved gods and goddesses, its strutting birds and prancing animals could have survived the years and man's indifference. It should have been declared a museum. For a while, a brilliant French savant, master of the National Centre of Scientific Research in Paris, Corneille Jest, made the courtyard an object of his concern. He encouraged interest in the building. He wrote informed papers which will meet the needs of future researchers and students. So in a way, the vanishing courtyard will live. The owner was prevented from selling it. For five years it slowly sagged and splintered and fell apart. I was told one day by the head of the foreign agency that the window was finally gone and I hadn't the courage to go and see for myself.

The Hill of the Camphor Tree

On the top of the hill stood a shrine as old almost as time and near it grew a camphor tree. A saintly Brahmin who came every day to pray and make offerings at the shrine, found that the milk he offered was invariably stolen. Determined to discover the culprit, he hid behind some bushes and in time a handsome youth stepped out of the camphor tree and fearlessly drank the milk. The enraged Brahmin struck the head from the boy's body with a single sweep of his sword, then fell trembling to the ground. For there, before him, emerging in great splendour from the severed head, was a four-headed emanation of Vishnu. Instead of filling earth and heaven with his fury, the god humbly thanked the Brahmin for freeing him from a powerful spell. Since then, the Vishnu of this hallowed place, called Changu Narayan, is known to many as Champak Narayan. Camphor trees still grow on the hill.

Changu Narayan is one of Kathmandu valley's oldest monuments, as old if not older, than the other famous hilltop shrine, the Buddhist stupa of Swayambhunath. It must have begun in the same way: a place of worship and pilgrimage given prominence because of its elevation; a cairn of stones at first; a small construction, a shrine, a temple. Below it and not too far away are the city of Bhaktapur and the town of Saukhu, both prosperous trading centres in their time. Both

straddled important trade routes between India and Tibet. It
is easy to imagine their patronage extending to the temple on
the hill so that it became one of the most celebrated centres
of Vaishnava worship. It is possible, and there is evidence to
support the belief in ruins and rubble scattered about the hill,
that there once was a considerable settlement along the ridge
leading to Changu Narayan, and about the temple itself. There
are remains of what might well have been a royal bath and
platforms that might have supported palaces and pavilions.

The Hill of the Camphor Tree / **169**

Where a derelict school now stands, are stone and brick foundations of ancient buildings. Was it from here perhaps that Nepal's first great historical figure, King Manadeva I, ruled? An inscription beside the temple of Changu Narayan, dated AD 467 not only substantiates the legendary king's existence, but records his marriages and his exploits. It credits him with conquests to the north and to the east, presumably far beyond the confines of the Kathmandu valley where other warring kingdoms clung to mountain tops or luxuriated in fertile valleys.

Somewhere below Changu Narayan, closer to the temple, I suspect, than far from it, stood the fabled palace of Managrha. I have been shown ruins in the royal forests of Gokarna nearby which lay claim to the royal site, and have been assured by scholars that it lies beneath the old Malla palace of Bhaktapur. I favour the site below the temple where the remains of the bath are and from where stone stairs lead to the hilltop. All this, of course, is fairy-tale conjecture. What is known is that the original temple required restoration in the late sixteenth century and was destroyed by a fire in 1702 when it was completely rebuilt. Since it is claimed for Changu Narayan that it was the very first of the pagoda-roofed temples, its association with the celebrated Nepalese architect Arniko, who lived in the late thirteenth century, cannot be dismissed. For, it is believed that Arniko was responsible for the pagoda roof and that he carried its design with him first to Tibet and then to China, where he became controller of the imperial manufactures.

But Arniko comes late upon the history of Changu Narayan. The temple's greatest treasures are Licchavi (circa AD 300 to 800), magnificent stone carvings grouped and strewn about the temple courtyard as if they had been shaken from the original temple, or temples, to which they belonged. Indeed, there are some fourteenth century small temples, either standing or in ruins, about the main shrine. More fabulous than the others among these Licchavi masterpieces, are an exquisite Vishnu Vishwarupa, a lordly Narsimha, and a Garuda Narayan of such powerful simplicity it has been rightly honoured by being reproduced on Nepalese paper currency. And there is the pillar with its historic inscription, that once stood before the temple, crowned by a *garuda*. An old *pujari* explained how it was that the pillar now stands beside the entrance to the temple, with the *garuda,* separately kneeling on a low plinth, facing the shrine. Pointing to a stone stump that was once part of the inscribed pillar, he said that Vishnu, suddenly angered by the *garuda* being at a higher level than himself, cut the pillar with his *chakra* and toppled his worshipful mount. More likely an earthquake was responsible, though one wonders why early and subsequent restorations didn't return the pillar and the *garuda* to their original positions. Legend, according to the *pujari,* has a demon shaking the hill of the camphor tree so violently that it required the efforts of the devi herself to kill the demon and anchor the hill to the valley floor.

Once fairly difficult to reach, the glories of Changu Narayan are now easily accessible. A new road, climbing and meandering through still unspoiled countryside, reaches almost to the temple itself. Where it stops, a charming village takes over; cottages not old but built on ancient foundations. A pristine fountain survives, surprisingly spouting a modern tap. Sadly, the ancient *pati* or rest house beside it is being allowed to collapse. On both sides of the wide road to the top, more often than not, ankle deep in grain spread out to dry, are beautifully carved plinths, water troughs, and fragments of carving that suggest the glory of what must have been. The temple itself, with its heavily gilded and patterned entrance doors, its beautifully carved wooden struts, its guardian lions and mythical beasts, its metal banners and rows of wind bells and its bright golden final beggars description. One even grows to like the now mellow colours that trick out the wood carving. They seem to belong with the surrounding trees and mountains and the high blue sky and impart to a majestic, royal temple, a rustic charm.

The Jewelled Gift of a Snake God

 Always, at this time of the year, the chariots of the red god Machhendranath complete their rumbling journey through the city of Patan. The monsoon should be imminent if not already begun. Rain should fall on this last day of the festival as Machhendranath is, among many other things, the bountiful god of rain. There are many, particularly among the farmers of the Kathmandu valley, who believe that if rain fails to drench the occasion, then a year of drought and hardship may result. Many are the foreign observers who are committed in writing to say that no one going to the Bhoto Jatra, as the last day of the Machhendranath festival is known, should fail to carry an umbrella, however bright the morning skies may be. This year, though rain threatened, not a drop fell.

We have met the red Machhendranath in these columns before: the benign. In god who was brought from Assam in the form of a black bee in a golden water vessel. He took up residence in a village called Bungamati where his five foot, scarlet image, traditionally painted by a single family of Patan artists, is kept until it is ritually bathed and enthroned in a great wooden chariot to be drawn through the streets of Patan once a year. The stout wooden yoke of the chariot with its gilded mask to which separate offerings are made, represents the snake god, Karkot, who helped to conduct Machhendranath from Assam. The four massive wooden wheels of the chariot are believed to be invested with the spirits of the terrifying Bhairabs who guarded the red god against the assault of demons on his journey to Kathmandu.

The tall spire of the chariot is a stunning construction of bamboo massively bound with cane: a tower so much larger than the chariot on which it rests that it appears to defy the laws of balance and gravity. Numerous ropes help to keep it erect. Decorated with foliage and flowers and hung with banners of cloth and gilded metal, it is crowned with a bouquet of national flags. The chariot of Minnath, variously described as the son or daughter of Machhendranath, who is himself attributed with numerous female characteristics, follows closely behind, similar in construction but smaller and apparently worshipped with equal fervour. Just when Minnath, who is more popularly known as Chakuwa Dev, became attached to the Machhendranath legend, is uncertain. He has no part in the entrancing story of Machhendranath's epic journey from Assam. Indeed, I had a *pujari* from the temple of Minnath insist that his beloved Chakuwa Dev is more ancient than Machhendranath, despite the popular belief that he is the child of the red god.

None of this really matters when one is part of the great throng that comes to make offerings to Machhendranath and ask his blessings on the final day of his festival. All Kathmandu fills the small space that was once a field where Machhendranath rested on his journey from Assam. Many have camped out the entire night, beginning their devotions at first light and feasting between their spells of worship. The ground before the chariot is bright with thousands of votive lamps. And now, modern touch, ice cream vendors and *gully-gully* men selling brightly coloured geegaws like ribbons, balloons, hair clips and toys plough through the crowds offering earthly temptation. Continuous lines of the devout

scatter rice on the chariots, offer *thalis* of food, and feed the grimacing mouths of the snake gods.

In the afternoon, the Patan Kumari is brought in procession to view the chariots and shortly afterwards, the king and queen, members of the royal family, and ministers of state, come to pay homage. This is one of the moments everyone has been waiting for because it signals the display of the fabled

The Jewelled Gift of a Snake God / **175**

bhoto, or jewelled waistcoat of Machhendranath. Old and wondrous is the story. The wife of the snake god suffered an incurable eye disease. Every doctor and miracle worker had tried to cure her, without avail. All hope of restoring her eyesight had been abandoned, when a farmer came forward and achieved the impossible. He cured the queen. So great was the joy of the snake god, Karkot, that he bestowed upon the farmer, a priceless jewelled waistcoat which stupidly, the farmer lost. One day, while attending the festival of Machhendranath, the farmer saw his precious coat on a stranger who insisted it was his. An unseemly argument ensued that would have ended in bloodshed had not the snake king, who was attending the festival in the guise of a human, intervened and given the disputed coat to Machhendranath. Rumour has it that the original garment is in a foreign museum and the coat now exposed to view is a copy. The excitement and unashamed emotion that greets the sight of the jewelled waistcoat or *bhoto*, as it is called, appears to disregard the story. This is a moment of timeless magic that mere rumour cannot tarnish. Genuine or not, the *bhoto* bestows a blessing on the faithful for yet another year, and I doubt that all the powerful ingredients of relentless change will ever detract from this ancient ceremony.

There is one more moment of special significance. An open-mouthed vessel is dropped from the very top of the chariot's spire. If it falls face down, then the people of Kathmandu valley can expect a year of plenty and happiness. But should the pot settle with its mouth pointing thirstily to the sky, then drought and distress may follow.

I did not wait to watch the vessel being dropped and no one I have met since seems to know which way it fell. Perhaps, like me, they didn't really want to know. The red god Machhendranath, who is also Padma Pani Boddhisatva or Lokeswar, protector and teacher of the gods themselves, had ridden grandly and serenely to his parting ceremony. If one believes that fervent prayers must surely be answered, then the prayers of all Kathmandu must prevail. I saw them offered and they were deeply impressive.

Tantric Secrets in a Deep Forest

 One of the loveliest places in the valley of Kathmandu is the forested hill of Chapagaon. An unmetalled road leads there from Patan, winding through terraced fields, small terracotta hamlets hidden in bamboo groves, and through two large, completely original villages almost carelessly stacked with ancient sculpture. The view is stunning. Great snow peaks fill the northern horizon, from the Annapurna, Himalchuli and Ganesh Himal massiffs in the west, to Gauri Shanker, Numbur and Everest in the east. Far, far below them, in a green bowl misted with smoke and dust is the sprawl of Kathmandu city, pierced with minarets and gilded temple roofs. To the south, and close, because one is actually climbing their lower flanks, is the high range separating Nepal from India. There is a time of the day when the setting sun paints them cobalt and purple and deep emerald, and their summits throw long rays of shadows across the sky. Then the snow peaks glow golden and pink and Kathmandu's twilight bowl twinkles with the first lights.

The forest is protected by law and superstition both: the reason for it still being there as few forests survive on the mountains about Kathmandu. One wishes this sure-fire method of conservation would be clamped on other areas before all the trees disappear. About the temple of Bajra Varahi

spirits are believed to live among the trees and certainly there is a feel of enchantment in the heavy shade and the writhing tree trunks. The pathway that plunges into the forest is soon paved with carved stone — petrified lotuses — that lead to the powerfully tantric temple. It stands two-tiered and squat in a sunken courtyard, guarded by stone lions, and though sunlight pours upon it through ragged skylights in the trees, it has a disquietingly sombre look. A gilded buffalo squats gazing at the temple from atop a stone platform under a metal umbrella. More lions, or they could be leopards, guard the entrance to the temple which is hung with brass bells. As I sit to sketch, a group of colourfully dressed hill people swarm about the entrance, ringing the bells and throwing offerings of flowers and rice into the dark interior. Suddenly a reluctant goat is dragged forward and its head severed with a swift flash of a *khukri*. The head is offered to the temple and the carcass is dragged away. The quiet of the jungle returns to the courtyard, the temple, and its company of deities.

The images, barely glimpsed in the deep gloom of the shrine are natural stone daubed with vermilion and now fresh blood. They represent the *ashtamatrikas*; Ganesh, Bhairab, Kumar, Singhini and Byahrini among them. The image of the goddess Bajra Varahi is also an unshaped stone, and though her companions are all Hindu gods and goddesses, she herself is tantric Buddhist, which is why this temple in the forest is sacred to Hindus and Buddhists alike.

Though records assure me that the temple was built in 1665 by King Srinivas Malla, when the valley was preoccupied with tantric practice, the site has a religious history that reaches far back into time. It is easy to imagine the stones in the temple once grouped under a great tree in the forest, that then reached forever. To the frightened traveller, here was an oasis of comforting prayer where he could make offerings, however humble, and beseech a blessing and protection against spirits, wild animals and, almost certainly, highway robbers. Perhaps, the trees felled to form the clearing became the temple. And it might well have been the leaves of the original tree falling consistently about the shrine, that gave rise to the existing legend of the enchanted leaves. Because the story persists that an unchanging pattern of falling leaves settles in the courtyard which, as it is cleared away, is replaced by others. The number of leaves never varies — no more, no less.

It was probably the proximity of the temple that encouraged the building of Chapagaon, the village outside the forest that straddled an old trade route to India. Equally possible, it was the villagers, ever aware of the brooding presence of the jungle nearby, who built the temple. For it is claimed that Chapagaon was raised by two Malla noblemen at the end of the tenth century. If this is so, then King Ratna Malla of Kathmandu, who ruled in the sixteenth century, merely bestowed royal recognition on a village already centuries old.

The more colourful story of Chapagaon's founding has King Ratna Malla being warned by his royal astrologers and soothsayers that his son, about to be born, must never look upon his face. If he did, the king would die. So the sorrowing king had the village of Chapagaon and a palace built for his unborn son, and there the infant was banished at birth with a retinue of attendants. Just outside the village is an old stone pool with traces of fine carving and a stone lotus at its centre that might have been a royal bath. And almost everywhere in the prosperous looking village, are stone images of surprising beauty that might well have been the deities of temples long since vanished. Part of the royal legend has the descendants of the luckless prince, surviving to this day, known as Babus. I have searched the village and the temple for a trace of these long ago royals, but found none. An old man, sitting besides a stone Krishna, seemed a likely source of information. Had he heared of Babus? I asked. He muttered the word over and over again, then looking at me searchingly asked me what they were. When I told him he cackled with laughter and shook his head. No, there were no Babus.

Alas! that memory is so short and even royal connections so frail. It somehow would have been gratifying to know that some distant descendant of Chapagaon's illustrious past lives. But, explained the old man, this village is better known to its Newari inhabitants as Wa. And Wa means 'the place of exile.'

A Divine Sleep in Stone

 It happened some fourteen centuries ago. Dislodged by a powerful earthquake, a part of the mountain called Shivpuri came crashing down; a vast and terrifying tumble of rock and earth that bore down upon the settlement below, completely buried it. Little could survive. Temples and houses were made of perishable mud and wood. Even memory was destroyed. The rains fell during their season and grass and forests grew. In time, men returned to clear the land unaware of the history below their feet. A farmer snarled his crude plough against a buried rock and when he chipped at it, it bled. In troubled awe, he cleared the soil away to uncover first the carved head of a stone colossus, then a reclining body and then a bed of coiled serpents on which it rested. Water began rising from the earth as he dug deeper, until it seemed the huge image floated on the surface of a pond. People heard and crowded to worship this strange god that had risen from the ground. It was recognised as Vishnu, but confusingly it was named Buddhanilkantha, which suggests Shiva.

There are other legends. When an earthquake ravaged the mountain, the image had only recently been consecrated. In fact the anonymous Licchavi master who carved it from a single enormous rock had hardly laid aside his tools when disaster came. Were the gods displeased? Did such perfection, daring to

transcend the bounds of mortality, arouse divine rebuke? Later, and even legend hesitates to say how long afterwards, the buried god appeared to King Dharmagat Dev in a dream so vivid that he was able to direct a search party to the spot where it lay. But the image was hardly uncovered when the mountain fell again and the reclining Vishnu was once more buried. When it was being excavated for the second time, a workman accidently clipped the divine nose and it bled. But one remembers that almost every early sculpture in the Kathmandu valley suffers a broken nose, a relic of the short-lived but savage assault by the forces of Shams-ud-din Ilyas of Bengal in the early fourteenth century. Legend also has an old Brahmin ascetic, Nil Kantha, responsible for having the image installed. But why, one wonders, did he give his Shivaite name to an image of Vishnu?

The confusion still exists. As I stood sketching beside the pond, my pad resting on the surrounding wall, small groups of Nepalese and Indian visitors piled up beside me and almost the first question asked on seeing the great image was 'What is it? Vishnu or Shiva?' Adding to their uncertainty were a number of Tibetan lamas who sat chanting under nearby trees. They made colourful offerings of ceremonial silk scarves and marigold chains, bouquets of incense sticks, fruit and *torna*, (small pyramids of dough stamped with impressions of Buddhist deities) and coins. A Nepalese guide explained to a family of Bengalis that the great image had not been made by man but by the gods themselves and he went on to describe how it had risen from the earth.

In the flurry of conversation that followed, a scholarly looking gentleman pointed out to one and all that such a wondrous creation was indeed divine. If they looked carefully at the supple chest, they could easily imagine that the image breathed. I was reminded that once, many years ago when carved stone fountains, now dry, used to pour clear mountain water into the pond, the ripples flowing across the surface heightened the illusion of breathing and I had watched fascinated not only as the great chest rose and fell, but as the vermilioned mouth smiled and the handsome face changed its expressions. Even now, a young man standing beside me remarked, 'See, Vishnu smiles; he is happy today.' And later, a tousled sadhu told me in a burst of wrinkled laughter that the god who was peacefully sleeping was about to wake. His eyes were moving.

There are always flowers banked above the crown of the image, and vermilion on its forehead, about its eyes and mouth and outlining the clothes and jewellery it wears. Vermilion stains the water of the now stagnant pond. Devotees mount a ramp to touch their foreheads to the massive feet, collecting some fragment of offerings made by others before them. In turn, they offer flowers and rice and coins that others will collect. Pujaris bathe and anoint the great face. More vermilion. Dramatic touches of saffron. There are always pigeons to accept the rice that is offered.

Yet another legend attaches to Buddhanilkantha. King Pratap Malla, who ruled in the seventeenth century, dreamed that if he or any of his descendants gazed upon the face of the reclining Vishnu, they would die. So no ruling monarch may visit this famed place of pilgrimage, but to allow them some idea of what they are forbidden to see, two similar but much smaller images were made and installed in the water garden at Balaju and in the grounds of the old Malla palace in Kathmandu.

Both lack the brilliance of the Licchavi original and the magic of its surroundings: the ancient rest houses and the hamlet of Buddhanilkantha and the fields strewn with black boulders like enormous cannon balls that fell from the mountain called Shivpuri. From one like these was the great Vishnu Narayan carved. From another, a Buddha image that stands unattended and hardly known in a field not far away. What other treasures lie buried beneath the great swell of earth that was once a landslide, we may only guess at. Nepal's leading public school and a rapidly growing suburb of Kathmandu reach across it. Perhaps someone digging a modern foundation will strike rock, and the rock will bleed.

The Temple of the Rising Sun

This is one of Kathmandu valley's many miracles: the treasured stuff of legends and fantasy that makes of a small temple in olden woods a place of great significance. The sun rises almost exactly behind Everest, sending rays of orange light across the sleeping valley. By meticulous calculations of court astrologers to a king of Bhaktapur three centuries ago, the temple was so sited that the very first rays strike the golden masked image of a vermilion Ganesh. By doing so, Surya pays homage to the powerful elephant-headed god and seeks blessings for his day's journey across the heavens.

There must have been an artist among those astrologers because the site is outrageously lovely. Down a winding country road, between a small changeless village and lush terraced fields, is the terracotta huddle of Bhaktapur with its temple towers and glint of golden finals. Beyond is the green and sapphire wall of the valley and the towering snow summits of sacred mountains. Though I suspect the ancient trees are slowly disappearing, the forest about the temple shades it with a canopy of feathery green. Birds sing in a never-ending chorus and cicadas shrill in competitive metallic sounds. There is now a broad stairway through the trees built by an early Rana prime minister that pauses every here and there, beside an image or

shrine. An impious thought perhaps, but maybe, like me, he found it necessary to rest on the long haul up the hill.

Built on a small platform scooped from the hillside, the temple has a shikhara type tower crowned by a golden finial from which gilded and plumed serpents hang defensively. Like so many temple serpents of this kind they are believed to breathe fire on occasion which only the most devout of pilgrims can see. So I thought it brave of a pujari to admit that he had never witnessed the phenomenon.

Beside the main image of Ganesh, set in a niche, incongruously patterned with art nouveau tiles and shaded by a gilded canopy, is a naturally shaped rock stained red with vermilion and the blood of sacrifice. Two gilded arches, deeply patterned with legendary beasts and *apsaras* that culminate in a canopy of serpents' heads, frame the image which is guarded by several stone and metal lions. A king gifted the large ceremonial bell to Surya Vinayak. Two devotees donated the gilded arches. Hundreds of visitors seeking divine favours have offered bells that hang in great profusion about the shrine and, a more recent and touchingly human innovation, scores of mere mortals seek immortality by hanging framed photographs of themselves on a nearby building.

Who, one wonders, offered the pair of late Victorian water hydrants embossed with the British lion that stand rather grandly on either side of the main shrine? They look strangely at home among the clutter of votive images, lamps, railings, bells, lions, and the compulsory shrew that stands devotedly atop a stone pillar with lotus capitals. No one seems to know for certain, but the two stone figures that kneel before the deity are probably King Vishnu Deva Varma, who built the temple, and his queen.

Of recent years it has become fashionable to be married at Surya Vinayak. There could be few lovelier places at which to make one's vows, particularly if the ceremony is blessed by that first ray of light that Surya bestows upon this renowned Ganesh. But the families who mostly throng the temple are praying for the wellbeing of their offspring, for Surya Vinayak has the reputation for curing retarded children, particularly those who show signs of being dumb.

Like so many of Kathmandu valley's temples that claim their origin to the patronage of some king, Surya Vinayak is certainly older than the building gifted by King Vishnu Deva Varma three centuries ago. It is a tantric shrine that in all probability was worshipped when the valley dwellers first penetrated the dense forests about Bhaktapur in search of wood or the sacred trees from which their ceremonial chariots are made. There was the rock that looked like a Ganesh, where sacrifice and prayer propitiated the jungle spirits. Perhaps even then, the first rays of the rising sun were seen to fall upon the stone. It was invested with magical properties. When word reached the royal court and the king, not above superstition and the need for miracles, a temple was planned and a place of quiet worship became a centre of public pilgrimage.

Children gather to watch me sketching, pronouncing my efforts *bala* or *bamla*. When I sketch a man sitting by a lion, they inform him in chorus that he is being portrayed and he strikes an indifferent pose. Several block my view in attitudes of Amitabh Bachchan or Mithun Chakravarty, hoping to be drawn until some thoughtful elder drives them away. A woman carries an infant to the shrine and stooping, touches vermilion from the feet of the god to the child's forehead. Her husband, a man of obvious importance dressed in a safari suit, walks about drinking Coca-Cola. From the verandah of the adjoining house, with its veneer of framed photographs, a group of men start singing *bhajans.*

The shadow of the hill above the temple throws its shadow across the valley. Surya has almost completed his journey and Ganesh settles to sleep. I feel horribly insignificant as I think of all the never-ending tomorrows when the first light of morning will ask its blessings of Surya Vinayak.

The Gorge of the Flaming Sword

 In the high wall of the Kathmandu valley, at a place called Chobar, is the gorge of legend. For here, when gods walked the earth and miracles were commonplace, the Mongolian saint Manjushri cut the mountain side with his flaming sword to drain a lake that filled the valley. His two wives, who he sat atop nearby summits, watched the awesome feat, matched only perhaps by the dividing of the waters of the Red Sea by Moses. Manjushri's motive was to reach and worship a lotus of incomparable beauty that floated upon the lake. Perhaps he also realized the rich potential of the valley that would result, for legend has him leaving his followers behind to found a city called Manjupatan.

That would be the end of the fable except that, like all fables it varies at every telling and is still in the process of being spun. So it was not Manjushri but Krishna who made the gorge by striking at the mountain with a thunderbolt. The thunderbolt assumed the shape of Ganesh, and is there below the gorge today, enshrined in a golden roofed temple, a strangely shapeless deity, and yet distinctly a Ganesh without a trunk. Fable comes forward immediately to explain, that before the temple was built, an innocent farmer while harvesting his corn, sliced off the trunk of the sleeping Ganesh.

There was a time not long ago when it was easier to fantasize about the gorge. It was Kathmandu's favourite picnic spot. Stood under tall old trees above the river that thundered through the narrow fault, there was the whole Kathmandu valley spread out below one, a bowl of emerald or gold or tawny green according to the season, and beyond the misted city with its gilded spires and pagoda roofs, the high steps of mountain ridges reaching to the snows. A wondrous sight one never tired of seeing. On the Kathmandu side of the hill were the loveliest rocks that may have been fashioned by a Japanese craftsman. Indeed the entire area, with its trees and shrubs gnarled and shaped by the winds that buffet the gorge, could have been designed by a Japanese master gardener. One spread one's picnic among the rocks and having fed, lay back to watch the changing light transform the valley and the towering snow summits with fleeting designs and colours: a temple roof vying briefly with a snow pyramid, the river Baghmati running silver though a purple landscape while the snows turned to gold.

Now a cement factory below the gorge is greedily eating the hill of fable. The beautiful rocks have been chewed to gravel. Many of the lovely trees have gone and often a pall of smoke or dust or both hangs over the area. One does not picnic anymore, but there is still the fantastic gorge to explore; narrow as a knife cut and as deep as the thrust of a powerful blade. Carved into its rocky walls, which themselves are masterpieces of natural sculpture, are numerous caves which legend has leading to a temple on top of the hill, to the city of Kirtipur, to the great Buddhist stupa of Swayambhunath which grew where the lotus settled, and to Tibet. I once happened upon a Nepali Brahmin sat beside a cave, which he assured me was full of treasure. He had seen it himself, piled about a pool deep inside the hill. He was prepared to share his discovery with me but observed that it was getting dark and he had no torch or tapers to light the way. But if I came during the day he would gladly conduct me inside. Everyone knew him. I had only to ask for Bhagwan. Somehow, the lure of treasure and the sight of a sacred pool, lost its appeal in the fetid smell of bats that belched from the dark cave with a regularity, that suggested an air conditioning plant somewhere deep down inside.

A geologist friend explained that the Kathmandu valley

was indeed once a lake: he used all the arguments of rock formations, types of soil, glacial traces and erosion that he emphasized with jargon to make impressive sense. The levels of its surface had been traced and the long process of its draining away recorded. He agreed that there were places more apparently vulnerable than Chobar, where centuries of erosion could have breached the valley wall, but obviously Chobar was at fault. We laughed at the pun. But far more acceptable to generations of the superstitious and devout, are the stories of divine intervention, and what followed.

When the waters of the lake receded, there were thousands of angry serpents left high and dry, the king and queen of the Nagas among them. They sought refuge in a small lake called Taudah that formed below the Chobar gorge, and some believe they are still there. More fascinating is the story that Karkot Nag, the serpent king who had been entrusted with the care of the priceless treasure which the demon Densur had stolen from Indra, the Lord of Heaven, hid it in Taudah Lake. So powerful was the legend that the first Rana prime minister, Jung Bahadur, is said to have had the lake repeatedly dragged in search of this heavenly wealth, but not even a sign of the snakes was found.

Now there's the cement factory belching pollution and one wonders how, in a thousand or more years time, it will be absorbed into legend.

The Greatest Building of Them All

Visitors to Kathmandu are invariably told that the great Rana palaces that rise like huge wedding cakes above the lesser confections of the city, were designed by French or British architects. Certainly they emulate the grand classical styles of Europe and are completely unlike the traditional Newari architecture of the Kathmandu valley. What comes as a surprise is to discover that the 'French' and 'British' architects were Nepalese, foremost among them the amazing brothers Kumar and Kishore Narshing, who were responsible for almost every palace of consequence in the valley. How they could have turned so easily, so conversantly, to this completely foreign style is remarkable, particularly as every palace they raised, either singly or together, had a distinct character of its own.

When the first Rana prime minister, Jung Bahadur journeyed to England and the Continent in 1850, he was deeply impressed not only by the extravagance of court life, the awesome military pageantry, and the personalities he met, like Queen Victoria and the Duke of Wellington, but by the lifestyle that centred about the great houses. Returning to Nepal he soon set about introducing the fashions of Europe into the Nepalese court. Military uniforms became flamboyantly Puritarian, ladies of the court adopted Western

hairstyles and wore their sarees in amazing approximation to crinolines and bustles. And modern palaces were built employing all the embellishments of Corinthian and Rococco, Baroque and neo-Gothic, high renaissance and Empire, and happily, an undeniable touch of Nepalese.

Having piled their extravagances all over the cities of Kathmandu and Patan, the Ranas' dream of raising the ultimate great palace as an official residence for the prime minister crystallized in the mind of Prime Minister Chandra Sumsher Jung Bahadur Rana who ordered work to begin in 1901. Acres of land had to be levelled, for what was to be a building of almost 1,800 rooms with well appointed parks and gardens all around. The rooms were built around seven courtyards which, beginning behind the magnificent façade, slowly diminished in importance. Here, in this amazing building considered to be the largest in Asia if not in all the world, lived the reigning maharaja, his numerous children and their families, retainers of various ranks, concubines and servants. Since retainers had retainers and concubines had servants of their own, there had to be a provision for them all.

The Singha Durbar palace is reached through imposing gates 'in the French style,' and up a drive beside reflecting pools in which fountain nymphs desport themselves. Bronze alligators yawn ominously on the banks of the pool, and pigeons forever preen themselves in silver painted iron. Great pillars, wreathed with plaster flowers, rise two floors above the ample porch which is itself embellished with foliated pillars, decorative urns and a marble balustrade. When one's eyes finally come to rest after exploring tiers of pillared galleries, arches, decorated pedestals and trees of wrought iron lamp bearers, it focusses on a large gilded lion, rampant, which holds aloft the national flag.

But if the outside is overpowering, the interior is incredible. I remember the grand marble stairway, the huge murals of the tiger hunt, when the prime minister was flung from his howdah to stand eye to eye in tall grass with a maddened tiger until rescued by his elephant. Gilt, priceless marble, Venetian mirrors, bohemian chandeliers, paintings and statuary are everywhere. Then, quite unexpectedly and uproariously is a hall of distorted mirrors as if it was felt necessary to include a touch of comic relief among such magnificence. I leave it to Percival Langdon, friend of the then ruling maharaja and author of a couple of the most fascinating books on Nepal, to describe 'the experience of shock' in seeing the great reception hall for the first time:

Its rich decoration may seem to many too rich, but it is only right to say that there is not in all India a hall of such magnificence. One wonders how all these enormous mirrors, these statues, these chandeliers of branching crystal, were brought over the mountain passes of Sisagarhi and Chandragiri. The heaviest pieces ever carried over are said to be the statues of the prime ministers. They weigh about four tons each... It is always said — though of course it was impossible for me to test the truth of the assertion — that the quarters set aside for the ladies of the maharaja's family are modelled upon those of Mortimer House, now Forbes House, in London.

There is a grand theatre, the Baithak Gallery, now used for sessions of the Rashtriya Panchayat. I have seen the overpowering Durbar Hall with its crystal chandeliers almost touching the crystal fountains that legend has playing champagne, used for banquets to President Rajendra Prasad and Queen Elizabeth. There could have been no more glittering occasions, as what jewelled detail had been omitted in the decor was more than amply made up for by the jewellery of the guests. It was incredible to know that all the sumptuous food being served in relays by liveried servants was being cooked on charcoal fires on a back verandah by Boris and his Hotel Royal staff, since the palace kitchen was miles away.

I remember visiting various government departments in days gone by when one entered, I think, the second courtyard through a side gate hung with the most tangled confusion of electric wires. It was a difficult job finding the room one wanted in that maze of corridors, all hung with skeins of electric wires. I recall someone once telling me that it was amazing the whole thing didn't go up in smoke. It did, in 1974, though the cause is still unknown. All Kathmandu turned out to watch and try to put out the flames that relentlessly devoured the buildings. I was told that many wept; that streams of molten crystal coursed through the garden.

By the timely command of the present king, Birendra Bir Bikram Shah, a part of the doomed building was dynamited to save the historic façade. It worked. And painstaking rebuilding has resulted in a new courtyard being erected behind the first. Others may follow.

As I sketched the buildings, a young soldier informed me that the Surya Bahadur Thapa government had just been overthrown and a new one was being elected. The water nymphs, I thought, would ride their silver steeds no matter what. It is important that the Singha Durbar endures.

Nana Sahib's Jewels Were Kept Here

 Having raised the spirit of Nepal's first Rana prime minister, Jung Bahadur, last week and turned to the amazing palaces of the Rana period, I went in search of Jung Bahadur's palace, knowing fully well that little of it remained. Some months ago, a friend had asked me to dinner in a small cottage built into the ruins of an original wing: a concrete box little bigger than a garage. By flashlight, he showed me the stumps of great pillars, and a few stone steps up which grand entries must once have been made. A Nepalese friend, in fact, went through the motions of several servile bows, so for a moment in the dark there was the taut, heroic general himself, plumed and gowned, offering perfunctory greeting. When I returned, looking for a fragment to sketch, a buffalo wallowed in a monsoon pool below the steps and there were no visions.

Another friend lives in two of the original rooms, or rather partitioned parts of one grand wing. She is reached by what must have been a servants' entrance and has a narrow balcony that looks out across the area known as Thapathali, after which the palace was named. The ceiling is high and between massive wooden beams carved with gargoyles at their ends, is a mat of roughly woven cane and branches. 'There was a painted ceiling cloth once,' she explains. Apparently this particular wing belonged to women of the household. If they still observe from some Rana heaven, they perhaps wonder at this foreign girl who collects tribal baskets and weaves and does her own cooking out of tribal pots and pans. A Rana friend of hers turns out to be one of the original family. From the small balcony, he traces the outlines of the old palace among ruins and a rash of new buildings.

'There,' he points towards the river Baghmati, 'was the garden where Jung Bahadur liked to walk with friends and confidants, not necessarily the same people. There used to be a bandstand in the garden where music was played on occasion.' Below us was a gate two floors high, blessed by the presence of a scarlet figure of Hanuman, and a little below it another, even stouter gate where the guard house can still be seen. 'Prisoners were often tied to the heavy wooden beams awaiting the prime minister's justice. The general himself lived up there,' he said, pointing through the walls uphill. Trying to follow his directions later, I was confronted by the seedy, if defiant, last stand of a rusty, tin-roofed building shorn of ornamentation or any pretence to grandeur. Here were the stumps of the pillars, and here two precarious walls with classical European windows that might well have belonged to a favourite study or living room. Their roof had long ago caved in; whatever magnificence they had once contained had been scattered ages before. Ironically, the walls stood smothered in a small fortune of marijuana plants. I doubt they will last out the monsoon and then the only classical flourishes that remain in this old palace will vanish.

An old engraving of 'Thapathali, Residence of Maharaja Jung Bahadur' shows a group of buildings raised on several levels beside the Baghmati river. At the centre is a four-storied, palatial edifice with a porch supported by classical pillars. Long, three-storied wings reach from it, while all about the grounds

are several houses of varying sizes. Along the river bank is a continuous wall of low buildings and ghats pierced by at least two well-protected gates. The individual houses are of interest, since it is known that Jung Bahadur offered asylum to a prince of Oudh and Begum Hazrat Mahal and gave them a residence near his palace. Here too he settled the two wives and mother of the fugitive Nana Sahib and here for a while reposed the legendary *naulakha,* 'a long necklace of pearls, diamonds and emeralds...perhaps without rival in the world', along with other fabulous treasures that Nana Sahib brought with him to Nepal.

Jung Bahadur purchased the *naulakha* for a take-it-or-leave-it 93,000 rupees, and set about adding most of the other gems to his collection. A stunning emerald, four inches in length which had been used by Nana Sahib as a seal, was incorporated in the gem-encrusted crown of the prime minister, as were a bunch of grape-sized emeralds. Clusters of diamonds fashioned into amulets, diadems, necklaces and rings all passed into Jung Bahadur's collection, at a price in cash, kind, property or emotion that can now only be guessed at.

I doubt that the old palace of Thapathali was as satisfyingly charming as the Rana palaces still standing, or as grandly elegant as the palace which Jung Bahadur had built for his brother in 1895 and which later became the official residence of the royal family: it owed quite a bit of its inspiration to Calcutta's Government House. Chroniclers of Jung Bahadur's time are given to describing the Thapathali palace as 'grim' and 'forbidding', but perhaps they saw little of the interiors: one wing just about standing boasted incredible murals until recently when someone obliterated them with electric blue paint. And Dr Oldfield, a contemporary of Jung Bahadur, describes treating a lady of the court in a pleasant room piled with rich rugs and fine cloths.

Which is all the more amazing that it has all been swept away so soon. Only a century, but then, a very long time ago.

Three Men on a Horse

All who know Calcutta will find the subject of my sketch familiar: the rearing bronze horse, the rider, sword-hand resting on his charger's flank, looking searchingly over his right shoulder. In Calcutta, it is perhaps the most brilliantly conceived of all the heroic bronzes of British viceroys and famous generals that once galloped the maidan and are now tucked away under trees in the Victoria Memorial or drawn up in some semblance of review in the old Government House at Barrackpore. This particular bronze, or rather its look-alike, used to occupy the traffic island opposite Park Street until it made way for the statue of Mahatma Gandhi. Where wags once offered the vision of General Sir James Outram charging up fashionable Park Street to have tea at Flurys and Trincas or read a new history of his times at the Oxford Book Depot, they may now suggest he is galloping away from the temptations of the street. In fact, he is forever frozen, leading a charge against the besieged residency in Lucknow and he wears the uniform of the Bengal Army which he commanded.

There is the magnificent charger, every muscle and vein faithfully portrayed, its tail streaming behind it. It requires only the slightest imagination to see the sweat coursing down its flanks and foam flecking its face. In Kathmandu, the rider is General Jung Bahadur, first Rana prime minister of Nepal, proud in all his decorations and wearing, perhaps, the legendary pearl necklace purchased from Nana Sahib. Queen Victoria had honoured him with the Knight Grand Cross of the Order of the Bath. Prince Louis Napoleon, later Napoleon III of France, presented him with his jewelled sword and the Emperor of China had bestowed upon him the country's highest (and most unpronounceable) award, accompanied by the Double-Eyed Peacock Feather and the Sable Coat. The general wears the gem-encrusted crown of the maharaja prime ministers, the bird of paradise plumes arching behind. His penetrating backward glance could be for any number of reasons, since Jung Bahadur, almost endlessly involved in plots and coups and palace intrigues, was forever on guard against assassination attempts as bizarre as any history has contrived. Pointing to a portrait in his place at Thapathali, he is quoted as saying to his companion, the British author of *Journey to Kathmandu,* Laurence Oliphanti, 'This is my poor uncle Mathabar Singh, whom I shot. It is very like him.'

A marble plaque set in the pedestal, decorated with the moon and the sun, a *khukri,* cannon balls, the imprint of feet, a rifle and a sword, bears the legend 'His Excellency Maharaja Sir Jung Bahadur Rana G.C.B & G.C.S.I. Though Ling Pim Mako Kang Wang Sian. Prime Minister and Commander-in-Chief, Nepal. Born 19th Ashad 1874 Sambat. Died 27th Phagoon 1933.' Surprisingly, there is also an inscription in Persian, and the sculptor's name, T. Brook, London 1881, is inscribed on the base of the statue.

Which came first, the Outram or the Jung Bahadur statue? Outram's obviously. Though the renowned sculptor J.H. Foley RA omits to add a date to his signature, an inscription tells us that the bronze was cast by R. Masefield & Co., Founders, London, in 1873. The general had died ten years earlier, so I wonder if he ever sat for his likeness. I had always taken it for

granted that both the Calcutta and Kathmandu statues were
the work of one man, but Jung Bahadur's statue has the name
T. Brooks, London, 1881, inscribed on its base: Brooks being
one of Foley's assistants, a brilliant copyist or responsible for
casting the second bronze from the original mould. Jung
Bahadur died in 1877, so once again the statue is posthumous
and one is left wondering how the sculptor arrived at so
detailed and perfect a likeness. Whatever the answers to an
intriguing situation, there is no doubt that these two almost
identical equestrian statues are among the finest anywhere.

Jung Bahadur wasn't the only Rana prime minister
perpetuated in bronze. They almost all were, and Kathmandu's
Tundikhel or Maidan, exhibits some outstanding statuary —
one achieving the almost impossible by having the horse rear
up on a single hind leg. Famous names in heroic statuary were

commissioned abroad. I know of only one exception, a sadly dispirited bronze of a later prime minister that commissioned locally, was considered too inferior to erect among its gallant brethren on Kathmandu's maidan. It stands, rather incongruously, in a temple courtyard.

What was amazing was the feat of getting these cumbersome and vastly heavy monuments to Kathmandu, as they belong to the time when everything imported had to be carried over the mountains between Nepal and India. Limousines, royal carriages, extravagant chandeliers, huge Venetian mirrors, grand pianos and suites of ponderous furniture all were brought in on the backs of porters toiling up precarious trails. Fragile chandeliers could find replacements for parts broken — mirrors must have been a headache — but how to replace a delicate finger broken or placate the bad omen of a decapitated prime minister? Carrying an elephant would have been easier.

There is a third in this trilogy of similar equestrian statues; that of Netaji Subhas Chandra Bose at the Sham Bazaar crossing. There is no doubt where the inspiration came from. A hundred years separates the original two and the disproportionate third, but there must be a moral somewhere in a single inspired work serving the memory of three such widely different but distinguished men: a dashing Nepalese prime minister, a British general and an Indian hero of Independence.

The Gates to the Royal Palace

 The old palace has gone, but the gate remains like a giant's wedding cake that the party somehow forgot to devour. In its fussy, faded white way it remains a monument to the great house that the first Rana prime minister, Jung Bahadur, had built for his brother Rana Udip Singh in 1847. For a site, he chose an area then outside the city limits, beside a historic spring and a famous temple to Narayan. One or perhaps both of the famous Narsingh brothers, who had been trained at the Roorkee Engineering College, were responsible for the building and they appear to have been inspired by more than one of Calcutta's grand colonial piles: a snatch of Government House which in turn was a copy of Keddleston Hall in Derbyshire, and a trace of the high court façade, sans stone.

Rana Udip Singh, who succeeded Jung Bahadur as prime minister, was assassinated in the palace by his nephews. Their motivation was simple. Jung Bahadur had decreed that succession to the post of prime minister would pass from brother to brother, then to the eldest nephew and his brothers thereafter. Which meant an inordinately long wait for those who desired the office. It is common in Kathmandu to hear reference to the families of Seven and Seventeen. Every Rana is descended from them. The seven are the brothers of Jung Bahadur, who after the murder of Rana Udip Singh disappeared from the official scene to be replaced by their seventeen nephews.

Ironically, the palace built by the first Rana prime minister became the official residence of the kings of Nepal after the murder of Rana Udip Singh. It was handsomely enlarged by Kumar Narsingh in 1899 and landscaped in the European manner with reflecting pools and follies, a bandstand and garden sculpture. This is how I saw it when Chou En-lai visited Kathmandu and was given a lavish reception in the old palace by the late King Mahendra. Red carpets climbed its twin marble stairways. Gurkha guards stood smartly in twin sentry boxes by the stairs and magnificent chandeliers blazed in the regal reception rooms. But no doubt about it, the old building trembled quite alarmingly below the weight of hundreds of guests. It was that threat of eventual collapse, perhaps, that prompted the tearing down of the splendid old palace and replacing it with a modern complex of uncertain architecture. At the same time as that was done, a modern road called Durbar Marg was bulldozed through parks and other palaces, to lead to the new front gate of the brand new Narayanhiti Durbar.

What perhaps the old palace lacked, the new one has in plenty — a limited but clear public view of the royal residence. Past the tall, wrought iron gates the royal approach passes through manicured gardens to marble stairs that climb to large silver doors. Above the doors is a tower of modern Nepalese design with a full length window through which, on occasion, can be seen the glitter of vast chandeliers.

Two of the original gates remain. A yellow concrete, art nouveau confection capped with white concrete snow, and the lovely old giant's wedding cake. I remember, when I first came to Kathmandu, crowds collecting outside the yellow concrete gate every morning for *darshan*. They seldom, if ever, caught a glimpse of the king, but they were there out of tradition and

the ancient loyalty that binds the Nepalese monarch to his
people. After standing about, almost reverently, for a while,
they would disperse as if on some given signal — voluble
again, smiling, satisfied. Village folk often stand outside the
new gates, peering in wonder at the abode of their king, while
foreign tourists pose for photographs. I never fail to feel a sense
of disappointment for them, because someone somewhere in
this land of the famous Gurkha soldiers, should have devised
a small daily pageant of changing of the guard.

While I sketched the old rococo gate, a group of Spanish
tourists persuaded the khaki and scarlet uniformed guards to
pose with them. A great deal of fun was had by all, as everyone
took turns to photograph the others and in an amazing mixture
of Spanish and Nepalese addresses were exchanged. I hope the
photographs arrive safely.

It was probably through this old gate, then flying banners
and bunting, that the extravagant marriage procession of Jung
Bahadur's eight-year-old son and a royal princess of six, passed
on its way to Jung Bahadur's palace at Thapathali. And
through the same gate, came a similar procession to finally

carry the bride away. According to contemporary records, they were occasions of great grandeur and celebration as cannons boomed and fireworks exploded in the Kathmandu night.

Legend has a king of old sacrificing himself, so that water would fill the new tank he had had built at Narayanhiti at a time of great drought. He chose his eldest son to be his unsuspecting murderer and it is believed that the carved fountains in the grounds of the Narayan temple close by the palace gate, turned their heads to heaven in horror. They are there still. And there is water in the tank. Perhaps, it was no mere chance that made Jung Bahadur chose this site for his brother's palace and no strange coincidence that had it become the residence of Nepal's kings.

The Kali of the South

 A bewitching drive away from Kathmandu, through the gorge cut by the Mongolian saint, Manjushri; past the small lake called Taudah where Indra's treasure is believed to be hidden and guarded by the snake king Karkot Nag; along a winding road that offers visions of endless beauty at every bend, is the most sacred shrine of Dakshin Kali. At one point along the road, with the whole Kathmandu valley spread below one, it is possible to see the dark pyramid of Everest among a whole horizon of bright snow summits. Turn a corner and the valley is lost behind a shoulder of mountain, the snows obliterated. Before one, the wide cradle of the holy Baghmati drops gradually to the Indian plains. It is believed that one of the reasons for the distant site of Dakshin Kali is to guard the southern routes to Kathmandu, not with the insignificantly small stone image of the goddess itself but with the tremendous tantric power the deity commands. As one enters a small, deeply forested valley where the temple is, that power becomes tangible in a brooding presence compounded of all the dark legends one has heard, and the knowledge that this small shrine is bathed in more blood than any other.

Stood at the confluence of two clear mountain streams, the water below the temple is often crimson with blood. On Tuesdays and Saturdays and particularly during the festival of

Dasain (Durga Puja) the small courtyard of the open air temple is ankle deep in the blood of sacrifice and Kali is continuously bathed with it. If, as I've heard it explained by a tantric sage, spirits flock to the smell of blood: scenes of massacre and murder, battlefields, and sacrificial temples, then they must throng the precincts of Dakshin Kali. As I sketched the temple, screened from the blood-letting by a wall behind the image, there was a sudden stir among those who idly watched me. A man who had just sacrificed a black goat and taken it to the confluence to wash and prepare for a family feast, had suddenly fallen to the ground, begun vomiting blood and died. The spirits had claimed him, said a young, grave-faced boy who was the son of a temple priest. It often happened, he said. The spirits lived in the trees and under rocks, and sometimes entering the temple claimed a victim. Was he not afraid? I asked. He evaded the question, as if an answer might provoke the very fear he was trying to hide.

Like so many of Kathmandu's temples, Dakshin Kali evolved from the dream of a Malla king who ruled in the fourteenth century. The Goddess Kali appeared to him in all her terrifying glory and commanded that he build a temple for her at a then unknown, unvisited spot. Immediately it was done, and one of many legends has those who sought the sacred place found it already marked by a stone image of the goddess. They left her open to the elements she commanded, but erected a gilded canopy supported by four golden serpents above her head. For company, she has images of Ganesh, seven *ashtamatrikas* and a free shaped stone Bhairab. Above the temple, approached by a forest path, is a still more simple temple dedicated to Kali's mother.

The great importance of Dakshin Kali lies in the ability of the goddess to make wishes come true and bless vows made with each sacrifice. Lovers, students, politicians, businessmen, gamblers, the childless and job seekers are among the hundreds

that visit the temple every week. Like the man who suddenly died after making his sacrifice, there may be those who come to wish release from sickness and pain. The small, black, stone goddess hears them all. A titled English lady I conducted to the shrine braved the gore to make a small offering to the goddess. She confessed to me later, that she had made a wish 'though naturally I don't for a moment believe in this sort of thing.' When I met her a couple of years later, she had been divorced after long years of marriage, so I wondered what her wish had been, and whether it had been answered or not.

There are rest houses about the temple and on the slopes above are grassy forest clearings where more light-hearted *pujas* are held and worshippers picnic off their sacrificed animals. An Indian friend of mine chose one of these charming spots in which to marry his French wife. Though the ancient Hindu ritual was correct and colourful and charged with emotion, the atmosphere was festive. Guests lounged on the grass, shaded from the brilliant sunshine by parasols or bunches of leaves. There were multicoloured paper flags and flowers on a pyramid of bamboos over the sacred fire. A Frenchman who had spent years learning to play the sitar and sing *bhajans,* played and sang in three languages — Hindi, French and English. Perhaps, below us, the confluence ran blood — we could not see it — but upon this sun-drenched hillside only the bride wore red, and if dark ghosts happened by, they were quickly converted by the joyous spirit of the occasion.

A Cow Festival to Honour the Dead

The monsoon is all but spent. The clouds no longer squat dark and unmoving on the Kathmandu valley, raining with a determined intensity. Now they hang softly about, are often swept from a dazzling sky, or sometimes gather suddenly to pour at random. Thousands of gossamer dragonflies sail on golden wings in the sunlight. The bamboo orchids bloom mauve and purple. There is a feel of autumn — the Nepalese will say winter — in the early morning air. And autumn means festivals. They line up out there in the near future like eagerly expected visitors, so near one can almost hear their chatter and see the gleam of their fine clothes.

One has just arrived, and gone, though its celebration has been prolonged in places where it seems the people are reluctant to let it go. These symptoms of reluctance are hardly peculiar to Nepal: I remember how every year in Calcutta an excuse was found to delay the departure of the Goddess Durga, so that one came upon pandals still occupied like late lamps attracting ever-eager moths, or saw small, enthusiastic immersions long after the splendidly riotous night of Bijoya Dashami. Here it is the festival of Gai Jatra, the procession of sacred cows, that honours the recently dead which may appear a strange reason for celebration, but then again, what a charming way to be remembered. There is lamentation and consoling prayer, mostly among the elderly and old, and the seriousness of ritual, but the mood of Gai Jatra is predominantly festive, as if in frolic the finality of death itself is being mocked, while living is celebrated. For who doesn't know that Yama Raj, the God of Death, sits in judgement on all souls, deciding which are to be admitted to the gates of *patal,* the underworld, and which are to find rebirth? The gates of *patal* are open only once a year and it often requires the assistance of a holy cow to push them open with its horns, just as departed souls require the guidance of a cow to show them the way. For, the journey through the underworld is fraught with the most terrifying of obstacles: rivers of fire, great valleys of ice, endless seas, deserts, enchanted forests infested with demons and spirits, blinding lights and temptations that can turn souls from salvation. The holy cow, by allowing souls to clasp its tail, guides them unerringly to the palace of Yama Raj.

So families bereaved during the past year send their children fancifully dressed as cows and sadhus, together with the family priest, musicians and often a real cow, in procession through the streets of Kathmandu. Depending on wealth and status, some of these family processions are large and splendidly attired. Others are as small as a couple of small, bemused children can be. All must follow a route dictated by tradition and all must pass below the windows of audience in the old royal palace; windows at which the Malla kings and their queens sat to watch the revelry. It is believed that the processions provided palace observers with a convenient census of deaths, but I know of no similar festival that indicates the number of births in the city.

Though every city and village in the Kathmandu valley has its Gai Jatra festival, they vary greatly in their expression.

Kathmandu has the gaily attired young 'cows' brilliantly robed
and crowned with printed cow masks, flowers, tinsel and horns
decorated with brightly coloured rosettes and flags. Their eyes
are enlarged with *kajal,* their rouged cheeks daubed with yellow
and most of them effect a painted moustache. They are
garlanded with flowers and trail white cloth tails behind them
which, after the ceremony, are cut into strips and worn by
members of the family as amulets. Women, from almost every
house they pass, make offerings to the 'cows': fruit, sweets,
flowers, parched rice or simply a mouthful of water from a brass
pot. In Bhaktapur, the 'cows' are towering constructions of
bamboo wound about with cloth, usually sarees, topped with
printed cow masks, horns of straws, and modern touch, brightly
coloured parasols. According to their size, these impressive

contraptions are either worn by a single person or carried on a litter by four or more men. Portraits of the dead are displayed, and the processions after winding through the streets of the city, gather in a square towered over by the great temple of five stages, to await the coming of Bhairab. The fierce god is represented by a tall decorated pyramid of straw, and about him wheel the 'cows', their attendant bands and groups of dancers: an amazing finale to the morning's devotions.

Patan, the city of artists, has processions featuring boys gorgeously dressed as Krishna, Rukmini, Radha and Prahlad, and dozens of girls as Krishna's devotees. What exactly they have to do with the hereafter, I'm not sure. Whereas in Kathmandu and Bhaktapur the family processions move separately, in Patan they gather together and move as one, stopping every now and again to receive the prayers and offerings of the devout along the way. There are bands, a few brightly attired human 'cows', real cows, at least one masked dancer, and great copper and brass drums filled with stones that are pulled at the head of the procession. The idea seems to be to make as much of a din as possible to drive both evil and reluctant spirits away. For, many are the souls of the dead that hang about their old homes in the hope of returning to life. All they do is haunt the living. The noise of Gai Jatra exorcises them.

A splendid old man who claimed to be over ninety-years-old, introduced himself and sat by me as the procession went by, saying a little ruefully that the celebrations now are a shadow of what they used to be. In his time, great pageants of dance, music and drama were staged by the rich and the processions were as elaborate and glittering as offerings to the gods should be. Did I know the secret of his age and strength? He had married several times. 'Never sleep alone,' he said to the delight of the people crowding about us. But now, he remarked matter-of-factly, he had only a couple of years left.

Then it would be his turn. He waved his walking stick at the passing 'deities' under their silk and brocaded umbrellas, the bands, the wildly leaping dancer, and the great barrels of sound. 'Next year, perhaps.'

I wondered aloud to some Nepalese friends how long the tradition of Gai Jatra would last. Would it not fall prey to modern advancement? In answer, one pointed to a rich procession of 'cows' under gold umbrellas, accompanied by two uniformed bands approaching us. They represented the royal family, he said, paying tribute to the memory of the late junior royal grand queen mother. And almost simultaneously, the widely travelled proprietor of one of Kathmandu's leading hotels came to ask if his son had passed by in procession. The boy had recently lost his grandfather.

Taking Toothaches to a God

If one dares count the coins nailed to the old tree stump, or just the nails of all sizes from small to enormous, and gives up at the ten thousandth, it would seem that Kathmandu is one vast toothache. For, every tack, nail, screw or coin knocked into the shrine means a prayer offered for relief of toothache. Which is amazing when one considers the flashing smiles that greet one everywhere. No well capped film stars could flash whiter. But there is this old lady with her student grandchild, both hammering away with bricks. I notice the lady is offering something the size of a chisel, and the child just an ordinary nail. No coins attached, but a light is lit when the exertion is done. When done, which will the small shrine bless? One hopes both; the agonizing molar and the painful milk tooth. After all, unlike going to the dentist, it is the sufferer who does all the work and the toothache god who effortlessly decides yes or no.

Legend has the god Washya Deo, yet another manifestation of Bhairab, attending a dance recital near the temple of Naradevi in the guise of a tree. How many unsuspecting people, I wonder, crouched in his shade or burdened his branches as they too fell under the spell of the dance? The god stayed transfixed so long that he took root and when eventually he tried to leave he found he couldn't

budge. At least his disguise couldn't, so he slipped out of it as he would a shirt, and there the tree remained. A discerning tantric soon discovered its identity and persuaded the obliging god to practise. Over the centuries, the tree has crumbled. Now, just a fragment remains, sheltered by an overhanging tiled roof, and crowned by a crude coronet of oil lamps. Until a year ago, may be less, a depression in the centre of the stump contained a small golden image. Perhaps some greatly relieved supplicant removed it in a fit of ecstasy or a constant sufferer took it home to compel a cure. Now there are the millions of nails, many washered with coins; tiny nails, small nails, big nails, large screws and wedges of steel. Perhaps the nails compare with the size of the toothache. Perhaps there was a time when a convenient hammer was provided at this wayside shrine. If so, it disappeared like the golden image. Now one is obliged to bring one's own or find a brick or stone.

When the dentists began moving in, is anyone's guess. It was an obvious place to set up shop. They could either entice the suffering on their way to the shrine or collect them when their supplications failed. The shops are distinctly aimed at those who cannot afford the luxury of the latest clinics or the long wait at government hospitals. Sign boards shout 'DAAT' in bold letters and display painted pink gums and whiter-than-snow teeth in promising grins. There are sets of false teeth exhibited in windows, along with all manner of dental equipment that cannot fail to attract the suffering, particularly villagers from the mountains. One sees them, carrying baskets of fruits or vegetables slung from their foreheads, or handsome woollen rugs over their arms and shoulders, deciding which den of salvation to patronize. Often they are aided by charts, photographs of pretty women with pearly teeth, and pictures of gods.

The shops are open to the streets, the dental chairs often innocent of screens so that an extraction can offer the same morbid fascination to passers-by as a public execution. I am assured that friends of the patient are often called upon to help the dentist when teeth are tough and resistance tougher, but this is something I haven't seen. I have heard suppressed screams welling out of a shop front but cannot vouch whether they were the patient's or the dentist's. They might even have been the protestations of an old pedal-generated drill. Once, when queues at better-known dental clinics were long and late and I suffered a nagging toothache, I seriously considered going to one of these shops near Washya Deo. The white-haired dentist looked expert and kindly, but I funked the publicity and the ferocious array of false teeth piled like petrified bites on glass shelves. Sadly, I disregarded the toothache god, not out of disbelief but embarrassed by the vision of me hammering away on a six inch nail while traffic came to a standstill.

The area called Bangemudha (*banga* meaning crooked and *mudha* a log of wood), offers other interests beside the toothache tree. Across a small square is an ancient statue of the Buddha, standing without explanation in the main doorway of a house. Its simplicity of line and texture place it in the Licchavi period (AD 300-800). Not far away is the handsome temple of Nardevi, dedicated to the white Kali who was invited by a Malla king to protect his city. All about are old houses heavily ornamented with carved windows and doors of great beauty. In a large courtyard is the sixteenth century stupa of Kathisimbhu, similar in looks to the hill top shrine of Swayambhunath. This is no coincidence, because the stupa offers similar merit to those who for reasons of ill health or age cannot worship at the great stupa on the hill. Legend has Kathisimbhu built in India near Benares. When it was completed there were none found competent to consecrate it, until a Nepalese priest happened along. After performing the complex rites, he set out for Kathmandu. To the amazement of all present and those gathered along the way, the large and magnificent stupa followed him.

On the same street is an ancient window that in a valley of exquisitely carved wooden windows is unique. So unique, in fact, that it has been given the Newari name of Deshemoru Jhaya which means, 'the like of which is not to be found anywhere.' That should be enchantment enough, but just a glance away from the pristine window is a small temple to Kankeshwor, distinguished by a large, six-pointed metal star above its mysterious front door. A visiting Jewish general was emphatic, that somehow the Nepalese had appropriated the Star of David. He is not alone in thinking so, just as the swastika is considered an import from Hitler's Germany by many surprised tourists. These tantric symbols of great

Taking Toothaches to a God / **223**

antiquity are common to Nepalese design, but the arguments persist. An eminent Indian once pointed to a bosomy Nepalese Tara and declared it to be an Indian god despite my protests. Every person to his own interpretation.

The ornate front door to the temple is always closed. Entry is made by an unostentatious door nearby, for legend has it that should the front door be opened, it would require human sacrifice. True or not, I doubt that anyone is going to put hearsay to test.

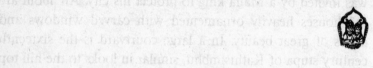

A Living Monument to a Glorious Past

There is nothing like it elsewhere. Nowhere, except in some ancient courtyard of Kathmandu, or Patan or Bhaktapur, or in a once prosperous village time forgot. And then, the similarity is only in style: the elegant proportions, the handsome extravagance of wood carving, the rosy sheen of old brick set one upon the other without pointing, the aura of antiquity. Mr Dwarika Das Shrestha gestures towards the façade and whispers 'thirteenth century,' which means the early Malla period. He talks soothingly and softly in the manner people effect in museums and cathedrals. 'Look at the door from here,' he says, selecting a spot under tall fruit trees, and I imagine it leads to a secret shrine. The beautifully carved window screens might hide ladies of a long-ago court, lovers or assassins of a distant past, or the merely curious of another age. Wait, and some sloe-eyed Juliet will appear on a carved balcony. More likely than not, she will have blue-rinsed hair and deliver her famous lines in one of several languages your Romeo might not understand. For, this is no palace, or stately home on the hill of thirty-two butterflies — or is it thirty-two dolls? — as the area is known. It is a small, very personalized hotel still in the process of being completed. 'It will be nothing when I've finished. Here, where this lawn is now, will be a concealed courtyard. Along that wall, and over there among those trees will be wings embodying the styles of different centuries. These large, spirally carved stones are pieces of a serpent pedestal. I'll erect it somewhere — perhaps there. And all those beautiful pillars and windows and doors will be absorbed in the new buildings. No two of them are the same. That's the beauty and wonder of them.'

We pause on a platform of ancient paving stones to admire what Mr Shrestha or DD as his friends call him, has already accomplished. The three storey building, raised lovingly among old trees — 'I hate cutting trees, don't you?' — is best described as neo-Newari: a clever blend of new design and technique embodying centuries' old masterpieces of carved wood. So the façade, because it has been built with the old, polished brick and is embellished with a thirteenth century door, windows and carved struts supporting the tiled roof, represents the beginning of the Malla style. I wonder aloud if the second floor balconies are not a little modern in their uncarved simplicity and Dwarika Das hurries me into a workshop where a treasure trove of old bits and pieces of carved wood are being painstakingly fitted together. Where sections are missing, exact copies are made. 'Here,' he says, holding up a length of elegant carving. 'Pieces like these will cover the balcony railings and those rows of new bricks that look objectionable among the old. They provide the required strength below the heavy windows. But they'll be camouflaged — there, like that there.' True, there is a window set in ancient brick that shows no trace of its transplanting. This is part of the magic of Dwarika's Village Hotel. Though comfortably modern where its amenities are concerned, it has a feel of age; a double-take look of having weathered the centuries. Even its interiors are liberally decorated with old works of art like a carved and gilded Rana ceiling. Painted

glass doors from Victorian England; a wooden window of exceptional beauty from a sixteenth century nobleman's house; terracotta plaques signifying achievement and failure, joy and sorrow, hope and despair, life and death. Interpret them as you will.

Conservation, not in the language of museums, but in every day usage, is a long standing dream of Dwarika Das. 'It's my life,' he says, his eyelids almost closing with memory. 'I remember being horrified to see people stripping old doors and windows of their carving, to make modern ones. They were chiselling away centuries of priceless art. So I gave them new wood in exchange for the old and they were very happy. That's how the whole thing happened. You know, people were so unthinking, they were selling their old windows — the country's heritage — for as little as thirty rupees each. My *mali* brought me two from the historic city of Kirtipur. He said there were many more. No one wanted them. They were being burned as fire wood and on funeral pyres. I wept.'

That was in 1955. With no clear idea then of what he would do with them, DD began collecting the abandoned doors and windows of an outmoded age. 'Slowly a passion developed. I spread my search all over the valley and as my collection grew, so did the idea of building a living monument. It was a dream. If I couldn't influence the youth of my country, I could save the ruins of our culture — the dead body of my mother.'

First there was the land planted with fruit trees. Then a small house, just enough for DD, his wife and growing family. Tentatively, he erected a chalet type lodge that seemed forgetful of his dream and his treasures. 'It was a mistake, it will go,' DD says. Then slowly, so that the swift rumour of Kathmandu hardly took notice, DD began building his dream house with the help of a few friendly architects. It was not yet done, when in 1980, it won for DD the prestigious PATA Heritage and Conservation award. In a few weeks time it played host to delegates of the Pacific Area Travel Association, Tourism and Conservation Convention, when they come by in their time machine.

That should be the happy ending to a success story, but it isn't. DD still dreams and it seems much work is yet to be done. 'I want to create. I don't want to go on holding a corpse because it is my dad or mother. No. I want to burn the corpse and start again. Create, or recreate heritage so that my son will benefit and carry on our traditions. I dedicate this to all those who care. I'm not taking it away with me. I cannot rebuild all Kathmandu but let this be a small nucleus for the new beginning.' Obviously DD means what he says. He has designed his own furniture employing traditional motifs; the *patra,* used in the worship of Vishnu; the Khadga, Durga's sword, and the elephant head of Ganesh. He restores old chests to become tables, makes writing desks from old paving stones, and mirrors from old window frames. Already there is a small amphitheatre for traditional dances and music. 'I'll improve it. Advise me. Help me. Find me people who are interested. Let me tell them about what I have in mind. Let me try and wake them up, inspire them. There is so much yet to do.'

A coach parks under the fruit trees. A small horde of tourists disgorges and makes for the office. I wonder for a moment as I watch their noisy progress who will meet them there. The very efficient Swiss manager with a shake of hands, or some brocaded courtier out of another age, with a deferential bow.

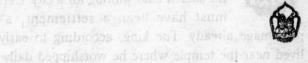

A Monument to an Indian Princess

 History is uncertain: it is a long time ago. Deupatan was either a flourishing city spread about the most holy shrine of Pashupatinath, or the sacred land waiting for a city. Certainly there must have been a settlement, a centre of pilgrimage already. The king, according to early travellers, lived near the temple where he worshipped daily.

There was a palace on a mound above Pashupatinath. And a road led to distant Swayambhunath on its sacred hill. Tradition, legend, natural surmise, has a sprawl of habitation about the sickle of the Baghmati that flowed through the Kathmandu valley. It was called Manjupatan after Manjushri, who drained a lake to form the valley. In the morass of time, dates have small meaning but a halo is forever cast about the time when Gautama Buddha was born. Scholars will forever debate whether he visited the valley of the gods or not: tradition says he did. He visited the city or town of Patan, where he bestowed the favour of his name upon the blacksmith caste by elevating them to Sakyas. After visiting Swayambhu he sat upon the lion throne made by Viswakarman, and read from the *Puranas* to the large company of people who had gathered to do him honour.

What concerns us more is the coming of the Mauryan emperor Ashoka in the footsteps of his master. He raised or

added to existing stupas wherever the Buddha had tarried or preached: four about the city of Patan, one on Swayambhunath hill, one at Boudhanath and one at Kirtipur.

There exist other stupas that may be Ashokan, overlooked by historians and scholars both. One is on the hill of the thirty-two butterflies, not far from Pashupatinath, another beside the new ring road below Swayambhunath and a third to the north of Bhaktapur. But even these are outside the limits of my concern with Ashoka's daughter Charumati.

They merely substantiate the visit to the Kathmandu valley of her forever famous father.

She must have travelled with him, and either it was love, a political arrangement or a strange fascination that had her married to a prince, Devapala, who is historically connected with Deupatan, near Pashupatinath. Hearsay history has him either living in the palace above the temple and administering the township of Deupatan, or founding it together with Charumati.

One fairly authenticated version of shadowy history has the impetuous Charumati — her beauty, her graces are left to imagination — deeply impressed by a display of sorcery and black magic. Water was turned to oil, water burned, an iron arrowhead was changed to stone and a wooden staff into a writhing snake. The Indian princess begged her father to marry her to the young prince Devapala — handsome, courageous, himself possessed of mystic powers?

It was done, and Charumati remained in her new homeland, helping to found not just one new town but two, because beside Deupatan she herself lavished patronage on a Buddhist settlement called Chabahil. There, inspired by her father, she raised a stupa and about it a *vihara*. Apparently she herself took more and more to a religious way of life and finally renouncing regal living, became a nun.

My sketch is of the Charumati vihar or *bahal* as it is today: old, very old but obviously not original. Perhaps it stands on ancient foundations, for the people of Chabahil are firm in their belief that it was Charumati who built it. The *pujari* doesn't even know who Charumati was: a goddess, he told me.

Three shrines occupy the square building. Beside the entrance, in the spirit of Buddhist-Hindu coexistence, is a small shrine to Bhairab, the terrifying protector. The main shrine is occupied by a standing Avalokeshwar, and immediately above, in a shrine forbidden to most visitors, is an Ajima, or grandmother goddess worshipped by Buddhists and Hindus alike.

Before the main shrine is a *chaitya* carved with four Buddhas that date to earliest Licchavi times (AD 300-800). Although still remarkably preserved, this historic monument is in urgent need of restoration. The *pujari* told me that some foreigners — he thought Americans — had come some years ago with promises to repair the building, but they never returned.

Nearby is the stupa Charumati built, painted with large, all-seeing eyes and surrounded by small votive *chaityas,* stupas and images. A beautiful Licchavi Buddha that had stood out the centuries, was briefly stolen but returned. All trace of the monastery that stood about the shrine has disappeared. Modern building begins to encroach upon the old Chabahil and its ancient neighbour Deupatan, are but names; only a few old buildings indicate where they once stood: in Chabahil, the stupa and the courtyard named after Charumati; in Deupatan, a tantric temple and a stone bath fed by carved water spouts where the prince and princess might once have bathed, and some ancient paving stones.

There is still the strong sense of tantric mysticism that attracted Charumati to the place. Legend has it that a tantric sage was locked for days in religious debate with a visiting Shankaracharya from south India in the small courtyard of an existing temple courtyard. The debate ended only when the Shankaracharya discovered that the temple goddess herself was aiding the tantric sage. And residents of the area are given to saying that they hear strange and often terrifying noises in the night, coming from the direction of a tantric shrine that now stands beside the new highway that rings the Kathmandu valley. Perhaps in the solemn and darkest darkness of the night, sorcerers still meet to change metal into stone and water into burning oil.

When Indra Was Caught Stealing

 Imagine Amitabh Bachchan in heavy disguise, a *burkha* perhaps, riding down Dharamtalla Street with not a glance in his direction. Then, choosing a maximum crowd at the Eden Garden stadium, he is suddenly transformed into the glittering superstar he is, decked out in something natty, his personality blazing. The crowd howls, stampedes. The football players run for their lives. When it appears that Mr Bachchan will be trampled into a rather unglamourous pulp, he is whisked away by his levitating mum who appeases the crowd by assuring them of free seats at every one of her son's movies that year, a promise impossible to keep. Now Mr Bachchan, for all his fame and good looks, is a mere mortal. How much more amazing the descent of a god from heaven, dressed in peasant's clothes and bent on a very human pursuit, like stealing flowers. The deity concerned was no ordinary god. He was Indra, the Lord of Heaven. When he descended on Kathmandu wrapped in a concealing cloud, no one recognized him. So much so that when he was discovered gathering *parijat* flowers, people caught and bound him hand and foot like a common thief.

For reasons best known to himself, Indra refused to reveal his identity and none suspected it even though his celestial elephant began searching the streets of Kathmandu for him. In heaven, Indra's mother, who had required the *parijat* flowers

Kumari

Indra captive

Indra's elephant

dīp

for the observance of a festival, grew so anxious at her son's disappearance, also descended on Kathmandu and lost no time in letting it be known who she and her son were. Great was the people's rejoicing and, presumably, their embarrassment. King and commoner alike celebrated their amazing good fortune with feasts and processions, song and dance. And when their divine guests were about to depart they asked a boon of Indra's mother. Would she take with her to heaven the souls of all those who had died that year? This she readily granted, besides bestowing a gift of her own — a gentle morning mist that would blanket the Kathmandu valley during

When Indra Was Caught Stealing / **235**

the autumn and winter months to ripen the harvest. Farmers are still apt to call it the gift of milk. As for the souls of the dead, she advised that they form a chain behind her holding on to each other, with the first taking a firm grip on her saree. Away they went like the tail of a great kite. They hadn't travelled far, when something as unfortunate as spiritual vertigo or fatigue, caused the chain to break and all the souls fell into a lake atop a mountain south of Kathmandu where bereaved families went to worship and honour them.

Right now, Kathmandu celebrates Indra *Jatra* which, fused together with the festival of the virgin goddess, Kumari, and the epic of the Nepalese king Yalambar who was slain by Krishna at the battle of the Mahabharata, is Nepal's most colourful celebration. Everyone, from the king, the royal family, ministers, government servants, the general public — even foreign diplomats — are involved. For this is the time of the year when the king receives the blessings of the Kumari who places *tikka* on his forehead. Superstition, well supported by strange circumstance or coincidence, enhances the belief that the Kumari, in fact, bestows upon the king the right to rule for another year. When, on occasion, she has mistakenly placed *tikka* on the wrong forehead, dire consequences have resulted. This too is the time when all the valley's Bhairab masks are displayed, particularly the great silver mask that Yalambar wore to battle, and the even larger, bejewelled golden mask of the white Bhairab in the old palace. All over the valley, in city, town and village are strange erections of wood, like wayside crucifixions, to which are tied masked dummies representing the captive Indra. Numerous images of other gods are brought out to watch the festival, for nobody, not even the hosts of heaven, would like to miss so wondrous an event.

Hung from a tall pole in the old palace square of Kathmandu is a colourful banner representing the flag presented to Indra by Vishnu. As long as it is there it means that the lord of heaven is in Kathmandu, bestowing upon the city and the country, his blessings and protection. At the foot of the pole is a small cage, both confining and enshrining an image of Indra and a golden elephant, his traditional mount. They represent the god's captivity, so many long legends ago. The pole itself is invested with significance. Some days before the festival begins, a government appointed priest and a select group of men from Kathmandu make for a pine forest not far from Bhaktapur. There, following ancient ritual and on-the-spot portents, they select a tree, offer prayer and blood sacrifice and after felling it, drag it in procession to the potters' village of Thimi. Men of Thimi bear it to Kathmandu's Tundikhel or maidan from where it is finally taken to the old palace square in Kathmandu by men of the city. There follows a blessing by the royal priest, who comes accompanied by soldiers in the olden uniforms of King Prithvi Narayan's Gurkha army carrying muskets and swords, and marching to a military band out of history. As the pole is raised into position, cannons boom and music plays. When the festival is done the great pole is taken in procession to the river Baghmati where it is immersed, cut into pieces to feed the perpetual flame that burns at yet another Bhairab shrine on the river bank.

So much for the living, for whom the Indra and Kumari *jatras* are carnivals of numerous attractions: dances representing the demons Lakhe and Dagini, enactments of the mortal incarnations of Vishnu, folk dramas, processions of masked 'deities,' a dancing elephant made of bamboo, painted cloth and human legs, and the massive trundle of the Kumari's *rath,* followed by lesser chariots of the living Ganesh and Bhairab, virgin boys selected in much the same way as the Kumari. And there is the king who can be seen more closely and more relaxed than at any other official occasion.

For the dear departed, are processions of lights and symbolic processions of men and women, holding onto each other in the way the spirits of old held hopefully to the saree of Indra's heaven-bound mother. There are prayers and fasts and feasts, and finally every bereaved family sends at least one member to the mountain top lake where the spirits once fell.

For those who like a more scholarly reason for festivals such as this, it is thought that the warrior king, whose Aryan forces overpowered India, inevitably turned his attention to the Himalayas. Perhaps the warlike hill people nagged his flanks. Leading an army against them he was captured and held prisoner until he promised some boon or settlement. The great Nepalese king Yalambar ruled Nepal at the time. No one less than a god, and the Lord of Heaven at that, could have fought and come to terms with him: an interesting thought as festival chariots roll through Kathmandu.

The Days of Dasain

The goddess comes and let no house be unprepared for her visitation. Every corner is swept clean, particularly the prayer room where the goddess will reside if her reception has been correctly planned. A vessel of holy water is placed in the room, and about it is heaped sand in which seeds of barley and other grain are planted. At an auspicious moment divined by astrologers, the family priest or the householder himself invokes the spirit of Durga to take possession of the water pot or *kalash*.

Extreme accuracy is called for, as the goddess will alight on the rim of the *kalash* for as long as a mustard seed can stand upright on the horn of a cow, and then move on. All things being done correctly, Durga is considered to have possessed the water pot, after which it is worshipped as the goddess herself throughout the days of the festival.

This first day of Dasain is known as Ghatasthapana, and already in the growing excitement of Nepal's greatest festival, ordinary, everyday living has changed its tempo if not come to a standstill. Holiday fever is virulent, causing people to take risks with their jobs by failing to turn up for work, spend all they have, or borrow beyond caring: village folk take off in droves for their mountain homes, laden with gifts and food for celebration.

Everywhere are herds of unsuspecting goats, sheep, and buffaloes, many of them imported from the plains or from the northern borders and Tibet. They will be sacrificed every day until they disappear in the vast blood-letting of Kalratri, the black night and the following day, Maha Nawami, when thousands of animals and fowl are offered to the goddess.

It is on this ninth day that the official military sacrifice is observed in the old armory or Kot near the ancient palace. As guns boom and muskets crackle, hundreds of animals are sacrificed and the blessings of the goddess invoked on piled arms and regimental flags. The Kot is accustomed to enormous carnage, for it was here that in 1864 the nobility of Kathmandu was massacred on the orders of an enraged, unbalanced queen, and a young courtier named Jung Bahadur emerged as the first of the Rana prime ministers who usurped the power of the throne for 104 years.

Towering above the armory is the beautiful temple of Teleju, the royal goddess who is another aspect of Durga. Here too is much sacrifice — some of the animals being killed in a number of ways dictated by tantric practice. On this same day, Vishwa Karma, the god of every instrument of toil, is worshipped with sacrifice, as is Bhairab, the male counterpart of Durga who, among his many functions, is the patron of locomotion. So sacrifice is made to machine tools and farming implements, to aircraft of the Royal Nepal Airlines as well as to motorcars and humble motor rickshaws. My driver demands money for a duck or more persuasively, a goat, which gives its blood to protect my minibus from accidents during the year.

On Vijaya Dasami or the tenth day of victory from which it derives its name, there is a final rush to the temples of Durga, a last minute offering of gifts to the gods, and a compulsory visiting of parents, relatives and friends. People wear their finest clothes, preferably new, and wear flowers or the young shoots of barley taken from the family Dasain shrine, in their

hair or tucked behind their ears. They receive *tikka* from their elders, usually the mixture of vermilion, rice and curd that has been offered to the sacred *kalash* in the family shrine. A salute of thirty-one guns marks the moment when a Brahmin priest in the palace places *tikka* on the kings forehead.

Then, in strict order of protocol, the king himself places *tikka* on the foreheads of members of the royal family, relatives, ministers, government officials, and finally anyone of the general public who wish to avail of this royal blessing. It is not uncommon to see foreign residents and tourists in the long queues that form outside the palace gates. I have seen hippies and a Christian priest in the queue.

My sketches concern themselves with the seventh day of Dasain, known as Fulpati, when the royal *kalash,* filled with banana leaves, tall grass, flowers, and sugarcane tied together with red cloth are brought to the Dasain shrine in the old royal palace from Gorkha, the ancestral home of the present royal house. It has taken three days for the colourful procession to travel the forty-five miles from Gurkha, a hilltop palace west of Kathmandu. Awaiting the Fulpati, which is carried by Brahmins on a decorated palanquin shaded by a gold embroidered umbrella, are a surge of highranking officials, army honour guards, banks, and throngs of people. There are soldiers in the olden uniforms of Gurkha, flute and drum bands out of history, singing men and women, swirls of incense and the bright eyes of flame.

On the Tundikhel, the king reviews his troops. Perfectly timed, seemingly endless volleys of rifle fire and the boom of cannons from the royal parade ground greet the Fulpati. Shortly afterwards, the king and queen arrive at the old palace where the Fulpati has been established, to worship the *kalash* and bouquet of sacred flowers. At exactly the same time, similar rites are performed in the old palace at Gorkha.

Under the Spreading Peepal Tree

On Kathmandu's New Road, one of the city's busiest shopping centres where the foreign goods are, is a large peepal tree. In its shade are a platform and several small votive shrines, mostly Buddhist that probably date to the time when an old Newari *bahal* or community courtyard, that collapsed in the devastating earthquake of 1934, occupied the area. The engaging old Rana general who had been responsible for clearing the earthquake damage, described it as 'ruins, ruins everywhere, piled right up against the old palace walls and as far as one dared to look. Like a warscape.' It was he who had planned the New Road and the modern complex about it, but he was not sure about the *bahal* of the peepal tree.

Perhaps there had been one. Perhaps there had been a temple. He would have to consult his old photographs and plans. Though we met again, the subject of the Peepal Bot, as the place is called, was forgotten, and then the wonderful old gentleman died, taking his secrets with him.

Today, Peepal Bot is Kathmandu's most popular rendezvous and viewing stand, a place where if you loiter long enough you will almost certainly meet or see people you wish to. Like editors of local newspapers. Street politicians. The relative or friend of somebody who knows somebody in high places; perhaps just the person who might help you find a job.

Here, on occasion, descend singing and pamphlet scattering devotees of ISKCON, contrasting with those who gather to mildly demonstrate for some reason or another. Here one might meet the self-styled Global Emperor, dressed in an antique black overcoat, black Nepalese cap decked out with beads and badges and carrying a tattered file filled with dictates written in his own hand on the backs of gods' pictures. Rumour has him an agent of some sort or another, a government spy keeping tabs on traffickers in drugs and black money or visaless foreigners, or, and this is the story I like best, the deranged Romeo who was denied the love of a high born lady.

He himself, claim some of the legends about him, came from a leading family of Kathmandu. He often stops me and in the most gentle of confidential whispers tells me that Krishna has the veto. At each meeting, I am enriched by a vivid god picture and one of his messages to mankind which he begs me to publish in the world press.

The Peepal Bot attracts shoeshine boys and hawkers of everything from cigarettes to snacks. Worshippers come at all times to make offerings or pray when there's no one about or to fight their way through the late afternoon and evening crowds. The platform is often used for Newari *bhoj* or feasts, participants suddenly squatting in circles under the tree, oblivious of the crowds passing by. Here people come not only to see but to be seen. Like the dying breed of New Road cowboys who wore natty denim outfits, high-heeled boots, hats or eye shades, transistors and Walkmans, and subconsciously affected John Travolta habits. One of them featured in a BBC television film — banned in Kathmandu — to the music of *Saturday Night Fever*.

That phase is done. Today's New Road cowboys, if indeed one can call them such, and a cautiously emerging breed of New Road cowgirls, prefer imported tee shirts, coloured neck scarves, and discreetly tailored clothes and hairstyles. In the winter it is down jackets or leather.

But mostly, the Peepal Bot is a meeting place for those who come to read the latest newspapers and magazines and discuss the day's news. There was, until recently, a convenient and well patronized bookshop just across the street, which to the dismay of the confirmed Peepal Bot habitue, was torn down and replaced by a slender concrete highrise, innocent of newspapers and magazines. Nothing daunted the hawkers who moved in, so one can buy every popular Nepalese, Indian and foreign publication under the peepal tree and find an immediate and informed coterie to share or argue your views with.

For years, a cafe that looks almost like a tree house in the branches of the Peepal Bot, has endeavoured to attract the potential customers below. And perhaps in recognition of all that concentrated reading, there are a fair number of shops selling reading glasses about the small square, and just a reach away is the busy office of Nepal's largest newspaper group.

Apart from being something of a Mecca to Indian tourists who on occasion can be seen picnicking in the Super Bazaar,

New Road is the ceremonial highway to the old Royal Palace and Durbar Square. I have seen the present king, and his father before him, ride to their coronations in splendid horse-drawn carriages, escorted by mounted guards, flag bearers, priests, officials, military bands and troops in olden and modern uniforms, to return leading magnificent processions of elephants. Every year the king passes by in a more simple motorcade to witness the beginning of the Kumari *jatra* and receive the blessings of the virgin goddess.

An imposing bronze statue of the Rana prime minister who had the road built, occupies a traffic island to gaze down the length of his creation. How modern the street must have appeared to him then, almost too wide in its absence of traffic and today's crowds. One wishes he could have had a preview of New Road as it is today, with its policeman chasing away parking cars that narrow the street, and its huge tourist coaches that require a traffic lane to themselves. Once they came overland from Europe, emblazoned with exotic signs and promising enchanted tours. The ghost of one still haunts the car park near the old palace. It was called the Chapatti Express. Whatever could have become of a coach with so unlikely a name?